D1560649

© *Alfredo Tucci*
© *Of this edition. Budo International Publ. Co.*
All the studio photographs are the work of Alfredo Tucci.

Graphic production: SERGRAPH, S.L.
ISBN: 84-96492-33-8
Legal Deposit: M-23.913-2006

CROSSROADS

WARRIORS

OF THE XXI CENTURY

ALFREDO TUCCI

CROSSROADS

What is freedom if not choosing? Every second in our lives is a crossroads, a meeting of various paths. Opting for one, we give up the time for others. Freedom is, then, an act that restricts us to a single direction; freedom is to say no to many options, choosing only one, and this is its greatest paradox.

Freedom silently encages us in that narrow hall of destiny where we have much less room to move than we would like. There, where the margin of action no longer has space or time, we understand that the first and the last stronghold of a warrior is his attitude.

But this is not an object of study in the lesson plans. There is no subject called "attitude". Attitude is the result of the sum total of the meeting of our essential natures with the world. Attitude is the greatest challenge of Being, and no one prepares us for it. This shouldn't seem strange since this forms a part of the world of content, not form, and in our times, which are far more of form than content, content becomes a bothersome excrescence.

Nonetheless, from its silent dwelling come the contents of Being that mark all the acts of our lives and that sow the paths of future men, societies and nations. Postponing its study, ignoring its power, is part of the collective suicide, of the general anesthesia in which we are, as a group, subscribing to.

For the Warrior, cultivating his attitude along his path is everything. The horizon of his excellence passes through powerful words like tempering, responsibility, impeccability, detachment, or fluidity. But these don't arise from a moral imposition. Morality is changing and its imposition generates an equal and opposite reaction that impedes fluidity. Nor is it strictly religious, since it doesn't require any intermediation in order to re-make ties. It doesn't provide good since that would contrast with some bad, yet it exercises it with the same naturalness as a fruit falling from a tree. The Warrior cultivates attention in order to understand, and in this way making possible that everything that occurs in him and through him is grandiose.

In the meeting of his world, a Warrior lives the crossroads of his generation and of his times, but his view is not the same as that of the common people. He opens sealed sewers, points out delicacies, warns of excesses, inspires at times, and very much despite himself, hurts at other times. The truth is always uncomfortable if it doesn't inhabit the center.

This book is the result of my reflections published during the past years in Budo International, which I am honored to direct. Each chapter is a personal voyage over the crossroads that I have been finding in our times, about the reflections that they have led me to. There is no intention to convince anyone, but I believe that it does invite reflection on almost everything that being a Warrior in our days involves.

It is our physical and spiritual obligation to return to our surroundings the products of our vital digestion since nothing remains in this changing universe. In this exchange with the surroundings, which we call life, what no longer serves one person is everything for another who requires it. As these words come out of me, they will no longer weigh in my interior; if they are useful to you, reader friend, nothing will give me greater pleasure.

Alfredo Tucci

"What is freedom if not choosing?
Every second in our lives is a
crossroads, a meeting
of various paths.
Opting for one, we give up the time
for others. Freedom is, then,
an act that restricts us to a single
direction; freedom is to say no to
many options, choosing only one,
and this is its greatest paradox"

PROLOG

It is not always the case that the one who runs the most reaches the goal, or that the strongest throws the discus the furthest, it happens to the one who always moves forward with firm conviction toward his objective. Self-control, will, and tempering are key factors in the life of the Warrior. He must be cold, calculating, and remorseless. Cold because he doesn't tremble in the face of danger and difficulties. Calculating because his strategy on the battlefield has been previously prepared. Remorseless because he doesn't deal with error lightly. In fact, he doesn't know how to live without honor.

A grand Master brought his disciples together in a large room and said: "The moment has come to choose my successor." He left for a moment and came back carrying in his hands a delicate and expensive porcelain vase; as he put it on the table, he declared out loud: "Here is the problem." His intrigued disciples looked at one another without understanding what was happening. For some moments that seemed like hours they didn't know what to do. Suddenly, one of the disciples got up and with a firm walk toward the table drew his sword, and with rapid and precise strikes, totally destroyed the vase, returning to his place afterward. Murmuring ran through the room before the master got up and said, pointing to that youngster: "Here is my successor."

At the crossroads in the life of a Warrior, one must do what is necessary to destroy problems, choosing the correct path to take, knowing how to define priorities. Alfredo Tucci is that warrior, one who has these qualities. A friend through long and difficult labors. A herald of the Martial Arts. He isn't afraid to speak the truth. A cultivated man, untiring in the techniques of learning, knowing, transmitting, and spreading.

His editorials show the culture and the great knowledge he possesses. His sensitivity has led him to be a great painter, his loyalty has made him a sincere friend.

I consider myself honored to be his personal friend and with this prolog to be able to participate in this marvelous work

Grand Master Mansur, 9th Dan Brazilian Jiu-Jitsu

PROLOG

Throughout time, great minds have indelibly marked history. Through profound thought, artistic accomplishment, scholarly research, sagacious insight and innovative design, these avant-gardists have turned the tide of popular opinion, challenged mediocrity and raised the banner of free thinking and progressive change. These are philosophers. These are master artists. These are writers. These are critical thinkers. These are those which challenge normalcy and cultivate greatness within their contemporaries. These are said to be, "before their time," yet those conversant with history know that these, rather, are "on time."

Having said this, I count it all honor to present to you a modern-day history-maker, Alfredo Tucci. Not only is this decorated martial artists and U.S. Marine Captain an accomplished writer, publisher, philosopher, philanthropist, and painter, but he is a man that does not shrink at confrontation. As the managing director of Budo International, Alfredo Tucci challenges boundaries, questions mindsets and stirs the waters of socially accepted stagnancy. He is a voice of profound influence and a person of great character. His goal, as with all of his works, is to educate, to challenge to action, to break barriers, to unify, to bridge understanding and to facilitate awareness. He is a virtuoso in his field and his influence spans the globe.

In his present work, Alfredo Tucci educates, inspires and challenges. His thought-provoking insight and skillful mastery of history, culture, and philosophic reflection offer and arm the reader with a perspective of today and a vision for tomorrow. I strongly encourage every martial artist, every scholar, every thinker, and every individual on a quest for truth to read and to study this profound work.

Like the artist employing perspective with reference to distance and horizon, so does Alfredo Tucci use perspective in identifying key indicators of change and progress. At the dawning of a crossroad, whether in the martial arts arena or simply in the arena of life, Alfredo engages his audience and encourages the innovation and application of ideas.

There is a saying that the pen is mightier than the sword, but this warrior wields both with equal proficiency, cutting to the core of the matter...or the man. To those who are well-versed with the works of this accomplished martial artist, the following pages will not disappoint. To those who have yet to make acquaintance, I present to you my friend and a man that not only possesses keen insight, but great vision and tremendous achievement: Alfredo Tucci.

**Grandmaster Christian Harfouche,
PhD 10th Dan, Shorite Ryu Tai Jutsu**

BUDO'S BIG SECRET

"The secret resides in the one who looks for it."

We human beings are a triumphant species. Our success has undoubtedly been due to our capacity to adapt ourselves as well as our capacity to impose ourselves. Both questions, opposite and complementary, are necessary. To impose oneself on the environment, it is necessary to fight against it, to conquer the territory from other species, convert their protein into human protein, and it is even necessary to confront fellow man, and in that way impose the law of the strongest, that same law that selected the best from each house from among us so that the human tribe was stronger.

In order to adapt oneself, one has to know how to "conform to" the environment, make oneself One with it. This implies understanding the laws that govern things to take advantage of superior forces in our benefit (the sail boat, agriculture, pasturage, etc.), but it also supposes an important dose of the ability to withstand, the capacity to suffer, and it implies enormous strength, incredible flexibility, capable of allowing us to live in extreme climates and in situations so varied that no other species has been able to emulate it.

But the wealth of man, accumulated throughout many generations, is being squandered in a question of a few hundred years. It's natural, everything winds up changing into its opposite with the passing of time, the law of change so dictates it. Natural selection has been substituted by social, and even geographic, selection for quite some time; no, the "pound of flesh" of an African isn't worth the same as that of a European or American. For the generations who lived the transition to "paradise," all these advantages have given them a comfortable existence, a long life-expectancy, and an enviable old age. But for the current generations, those who take it for granted, what they hadn't conquered with their efforts, the paradise is turning into hell.

I'm not going to speak here about the biological decadence of the species, but I will mention that the data is overwhelming: the increase of weakness (dis-ease), the appearance of new plagues and the no less significant re-appearance of old enemies supposedly eradicated (tuberculosis, smallpox, etc.); markers of the accelerated state of our immune system, like the increase in allergies; the unstoppable plague of mental illness; the loss of the effectiveness of antibiotics (the enemy is getting strong, we are getting weak); the appearance of new viruses; the growth of the areas affected by malaria and other diseases transmitted by insects, which themselves increase more and more with the heating up of the planet toward the north, etc., etc....

In this silent and non-bloody battle that we are involved in each and every day as a species and as individuals, an elemental and undoubtedly essential strategy is that of strengthening ourselves. For that, it is necessary to fight, and when fighting is involved, nothing compares to the ways of the warrior.

Martial Arts are one of those few formulations of activity whose effectiveness is more than proven, not only as a salutary lesson and stimulus for our bodies, but also for our minds and spirits, excessively impetuous and separated from natural experience to the point of taking as a given (and a right!) that which is not, rather the achievement of a conquest, of a well-directed effort maintained with diligence.

The end result is that the very fact of fighting has come to be politically incorrect. For the power, for the "shepherds," they are interested in the herd walking together, that it doesn't think, and that no one leaves the established trail. Fear is their tool, and what better way than to combine it with the belief that they are doing us a favor. In this situation, the clouding over is such that it is only comparable to the arrogance of believing ourselves the holders of rights that make us immune to nature itself, but for that we have present-day religion, oh, the all-powerful science! Come to our rescue! Wipe out nature! But there is no fooling mother nature... one can hold up water by a dam, but one way or another it is going to find its way to the sea.

Practicing Budo is a way of reminding us, from the most elemental perspective, how fragile we are, and at the same time it is a way to strengthen ourselves, a way to communicate with primordial instincts which, despite all the computers and cell phones we have, form an inseparable part of our essence as human beings. It is a way of recycling the excesses that our way of life inevitably brings: excess of food, of drink, of passivity, of self-pity, of information, of thoughts about feeling, of placing complacent emotions above all others. Budo reminds us that we are fighters, predators, that there exists a nature with which to conform to, a nature that possesses some laws that must be respected, that there are some equations that are balanced and others no, and when we transgress them, the consequences are not abstract, or legal, they are vital.

Budo is an amulet against many and very varied ways of personal foolishness: omnipotence (someone always winds up giving you what you deserve), boasting (there is always someone who does it better than you… always something that can withstand you), rigidity (either you adapt… or you won't be able to withstand), vanity (the mirror of the Dojo is an implacable witness), inertial (you have to train!), etc.

Budo is also an antidote for overcoming low physical and mental states, a softener of harsh remarks and daily tensions, and a balm against the fundamental frustration that accompanies the very act of living, since we all know that, despite our efforts to forget about it, we have an expiration date.

Budo deals with death and in this way prepares us for it gallantly, so that when it comes for us, it finds us fighting "like a cat belly up" but serene, willing, as Castaneda says, to dance our vital kata impeccably before it, knowing, at the end of the road, that we will not win that battle. Therefore, if we have walked like warriors, we will, in the end, have the ability to know how to give ourselves over contentedly since we will have discovered the big secret: and it is that the secret of Budo is not victory, rather "not being defeated." So, in the last quantum leap we will have conquered the power of fusing once again with the Everything that we already are.

THE EXPRESSION OF THE MYSTERY OF THE INVISIBLE

"Martial Arts". We are so accustomed to saying it that we don't even stop to think about what Art means. We do Martial Arts, speak about Art with capital letters, of the Arts, handicrafts, the artistic and the artists, but would we know how to define its meaning if some indiscreet and curious student (and there are always some) threw such a question at us?

Everything artistic is surrounded by a halo of charm and transcendence that is frequently disconcerting and at times turns off those ignorant in the material. This generates a certain elitism frequently poorly understood, an elitism that shouldn't correspond to any social difference, but rather on the personal level. Art is not a question of status or stock, it is, perhaps, an aristocracy of the spirit; however, the obtuse, closed languages, the ostentation behind what is hidden in the pretentious speeches of the critics, that meta-language with which they wrap this phenomenon, have distanced it from its true dimension, from its natural space, a space accessible to anyone (not necessarily intellectual!) that approaches it sincerely, with the skin and the five senses open to the experience.

For me, Art is the expression of the mystery of the invisible.

The invisible, for being such, isn't to say that it doesn't exist; nor does it say that all beings who participate in its mystery don't perceive it. It simply means that it is not in sight, that it remains hidden behind each thing, each Being, in the very make-up of the Universe.

Art belongs to the world of mystery to the extent that it is able to surpass restrictive definitions that want to put a value on it in function of aesthetic, philosophical and of course technical recourses. Art is not techniques; these can be the tools with which we approach it, but knowing the Arab alphabet doesn't necessarily mean that we know how to write in Arabic, and much less that we can write a poem in that language.

As in all that concerns mystery, Art is in itself a way of superior consciousness. Penetrating its language is undoubtedly a way of transcending ourselves, of going beyond our perceptive limits and navigating through those beautiful seas where everything is possible, a privilege that until then was only the assets of the gods. On such a voyage we learn to use creativity, that way of getting something from nothing, or simply of mixing everything, and the final result is new, and of course superior in value to the parts that make it up.

The artist is born, but is also made. Born to the extent that we are not equally gifted with the tools of sensitivity and of the necessary strength to first perceive, and later be able to express the mystery of the invisible with the same intensity. However, given that we all contribute to it (in the same way that the drop is part of the ocean), we can perfectly enjoy the expression of others as references on our path, as emergences from our own perception of the mystery. The artist, then, is in some ways a hierophant, an emergent from the collective. They receive what is being emitted with their antennas, "that which inundates the air" at a precise moment, in a specific place, and they are able to express it, re-written through their personal stamp. This exercise occurs not so much as the result of the virtues of the artist as from his defects, despite the fact that the majority of us think the contrary. What is certain is that the artist possesses the ability to express his "feelings", but these usually feed on his "deficiencies" before his "excesses" as an individual. The artist is frequently an especially unbalanced being, and it is precisely in his effort to reach a certain personal balance that he attains, by using his facets in excess (abilities), a better balance through his expressive work, his struggle to give form to the intense, vital perturbation that continuously alters the natural tendency toward inertia that we all carry within us.

The suffering of artists in the act of creation has always been spoken about, but what is certain is that the suffering is previous. However, it is conjured through this same act. This is, of course, like all birth, an event that requires effort, that involves a certain dosage of pain, of consciousness, and of a strange mix of will and abandon. Yet, the end result is not only balancing but especially able to contribute a calm pleasure that has no equal.

Whatever the Art in question might be, Art is there in order to serve the artist and not the reverse. The end is not the work, the result, but the path that its realization involves. The true achievement of the artist is within him; what remains outside of him is the materialized result of his conquest, not the end of it. If, besides, what remains has that rare quality of beauty and is capable of moving others, well... frosting on the cake!

In few Arts like in the Martial Arts the result of the conquest is briefer and more fading than our way of expressing ourselves. Like the Arts of Mars, our practices manifest themselves inconveniently, in the immediate, and despite their attending to matters clearly tangible and basic like self-defense, its artistic result is immaterial as in the case of dance or music; we are the very canvas that we paint on.

Like in other artistic forms, there are many levels of manifestation, an immensity of formulas to approach the creative and transcendent act of reaching and expressing the mystery. In its highest conceptions, the Martial Arts have the embodiment, significance and strength of a way of life that involves all of our Being, physical, emotional, and mental, in search of the mystery, in the realization of the ultimate Truth. In this sense there is a book that in my opinion marvelously describes this quest and its implications, "Zen and the Art of Archery" (Bungaku Hakusi), by Eugen Herriguel. I would like to finish this editorial quoting two of his many wonderful paragraphs, full of the deepest meaning of the way of the warrior. I hope that you like them and that they intrigue you so much that you can't help but read the whole thing, as happened to me, now almost thirty years ago:

"The spider 'dances' its web without knowing anything about the existence of the flies that will be trapped in it. The fly dancing unconcerned in the sunlight gets caught without knowing what awaits it. Through both, "It" dances and the interior and the exterior are one in this dance. In the same way, the archer hits the target without aiming exteriorly."

"If one feels irresistibly driven toward that goal (supreme freedom)...) he has to walk once again on the path of the Art without artifice. He has to jump back to the origin (and original) so that he lives from the Truth like someone who has integrally identified with it. (...)If he comes out successful from this adventure, then his destiny will be consumed in the confrontation with the non-refracted Truth, the Truth that is above all truths, the amorphous origin of all the origins: the Nothing that is everything, the Nothing that will devour it and from that be born again."

"For me, Art is the expression of the
mystery of the invisible.
The invisible, for being such, isn't to
say that it doesn't exist;
nor does it say that all beings who
participate in its mystery don't
perceive it. It simply means that it is
not in sight, that it remains hidden
behind each thing, each Being,
in the very make-up of the Universe"

RACISM, NATIONALISM, AND EXCLUSION IN MARTIAL ARTS

"All things become important at the limits, where they cease to be."
Eduardo Chillida (Sculptor)

Scientists have isolated a little fraction of our DNA, the DNA Mitochondria, a group of genetic markers situated in the periphery of the ovule, which, by not mixing in the nucleus with the genetic contributions of the father and mother, has remained almost immaculate from the beginnings of our species some 150,000 years ago in Africa. This message is transmitted from mothers to daughters and is perpetuated through them. In this way, the scientists have established a series of families, of "Eves", which come from the original in Africa, and which shaped "family groups" in areas like the Middle East, Italy, Spain, etc....

Through the analysis of our DNA, we can know exactly what the origin is of each one of us following our genealogical tree into its remotest past. The conclusions of this study, done principally at the University of Oxford, are extraordinary: There was very little differentiation among our ancestors and today the differences between us are miniscule since we all have a common origin. The races are simple adaptations to different climatic conditions but their origins have no relationship at all with belonging to one or the other family. One can belong to the family that comes from the Middle East and be white, black, red or yellow.

To know of ourselves with scientific certainty that we are all brothers must put more than one in an uncomfortable situation, determined to find substantial differences in their structure and ancestry, in their defects, and in their culture, country and even native land. When we look at things with enough perspective the same thing always happens, the differences dissolve, the common, the underlying sense of unity prevails and exclusion, in any form, becomes the simple nightmare of someone shortsighted, what a friend of mine rightly calls, small-minded people.

The Martial community is, generally speaking, much more open to other cultures than the average citizen of their country. This is undoubtedly due to the fact that the majority of us have learned to appreciate, through our training, the implicit cultural values in the difference between the East and the West. If your Master has not been Korean, Philippine, Chinese or Japanese (for example!), it is sure that the Master of your Master was. This led, as all things during their first and epic periods, to certain excesses that have fortunately been disappearing. Excesses that generated ridiculous situations and some, it must be said, abusive: I remember when it seemed that any guy with almond-shaped eyes had to be a Martial Arts Master! We counted the push-ups in Japanese and when it came to giving classes, we took our imitations to paroxysms and wound up speaking like we were Indians, How! You hit more hard! You not know well posture! You need train more! Etc...

On the other hand, some Eastern Masters didn't take pains to bring their Art closer to our culture, nor did they even know how to go about it; because many didn't do it, they didn't even learn the local language well. Some of them fell into the temptation of trying to control the evolution of the incipient national sports organizations and they did it with an iron hand and with absolute contempt for the democratic methods in practice; others converted their schools into private hunting grounds where they abused their ascendance over the students. Fortunately, we have been overcoming these and many other abuses and all of us have matured a lot since then.

Another form of exclusion in which some decide to fall is that of nationalism. In some countries more than others I have been able to observe little chauvinist factions that think that they are better than the rest... some write me lines like, "Let's see when you will publish more about the experts in our country, who are the best," or, "The only thing we are interested in is what happens in our country," etc. Or, "I think your magazine brings in too many foreign experts," and other similar compliments.

Fortunately, the majority doesn't see things like this, living proof of it is that our magazine is "alive and kicking" in a lot of countries and in seven languages, but it hasn't ceased to be symptomatic to encounter people who still make the effort to look for "their difference" through nationalism. When I was little and got on an airplane for the first time I admired the fact that I could verify that from the air the countries were not like on the political maps. In reality, those lines didn't exist anywhere!

In my opinion, exclusion, in any of form, finds its ultimate reason for existing and sinks its deepest roots in only one thing: fear. Fear of what is different is natural. The different is unknown, and the unknown, my friend, as much as it might attract, we don't like at all! However, it is necessary to know how to channel this natural tendency: as always, the solution is not fighting against the darkness, but simply turning on the light. One must learn and affirm oneself internally; whoever is strong internally is not afraid, since he or she knows that they will respond to danger if it presents itself. On the other side, the weak person, the sickly, yield to pressure and need to re-affirm themselves in some way, and better to do it marking a line on the ground, a border, a difference, although these are always an agreement, a formal framework, in sum, an excuse.

Patriotism is not nationalism (or it shouldn't be!). It is, shall we say, the positive side, the "luminous overleaf" of nationalism. Patriotism helps many people to visualize common spaces of that which they feel as "the closest family". Love of the land where you were born, or of the land that welcomes you (Don Quijote said, "One is not from where they were born but from where they graze!"), honors the one who practices it since through love of the small one can reach the love of the great, discovering that at the end, all is One; love (Eros), the universal force of fusion, dictates it so. However, those who can see the whole will love all lands and will respect them as one mother who is the mother of us all. Gea, Pachamama, Primordial Venus, Mother Earth, it is one thing with infinite names, a wonderful miracle in the enormous empty spaces of the Universe.

Today I began my editorial with the quotation of a great artist who I admire, the Basque sculptor Eduardo Chillida; he left us a few months ago. Like all great artists, his spirit brushed the infinite , transforming him into a visionary, someone who emerged from the collective unconscious, into a Master. I wanted to finish this text with another admirable quotation of this great sculptor, a quotation that is closely tied to the theme that concerns us today. I leave you in good hands until next month:

"I believe that the horizon, just as I see it, could be the motherland of all mankind."

FRIENDSHIP

"Once and a while life,
re-touched with the paintbrush,
makes our hair stand on end
and there are no words
to name what it offers
to those who know how to use it."

(lyrics of the song
"Once and a While Life")
Joan Manuel Serrat

There is nothing as noble in life as friendship. Friendship is the strongest possible union between two beings, a form of generous love and of respect without comparison.

Sympathy and synchronicity are two of the characteristics that most stand out in friendship. The classical Greek prefix "syn" means "with"; synchronicity means, then, with Cronos, "with time" and sympathy—with pathos—with passion. There is undoubtedly heart and synchronicity in friendship. The true friend, the companion, accompanies you through the years in such a way that one hardly notices the changes in oneself nor those of the other. He is always your brother, that chosen companion with whom you can be yourself, park the "mask" (an ancient Greek word for "person") and even laugh at it. The years that can pass without seeing him are not important, the friend comes back and finds you at the same point where you separated, Dicebamus hesterna die... the soul mate is timeless.

Friends are like two guitar strings tuned to the same pitch, life strums one and the other vibrates. I owe the best moments of my life to my friends, but they have also been the balsam in the worst. Their advice, as good as it might have been, was never comparable to their company, to their respect and to their sincere appreciation of my individuality. Each time that the biggest horrors threatened me, each time I was afraid, like Asterix and Obelix, that the sky was falling on my head, they, reading me like an open book, knew how to give what was necessary, many times simply being there, at the distance of a real hug, vibrating by my side and without stopping to be what I most appreciate, themselves.

My friends are peculiar. Generally, they are older than me, they draw their own maps on their voyages, maps that they transmit to me with the effort and detail with which a friar scribe decorates a sacred codex; and although each man is a unique path in himself, they advice me about those dangers around the corner that await everyone for the simple fact of being men. They are balloon probes from which I receive a reliable message, a wise warning, and exemplary criticism. When they were shipwrecked, nothing stopped me from saving them! When their boat got beached, I threw them my best life-jackets, whether in a bar or by a hospital bed, wherever it was necessary. They have me and they know it.

My friends fill me with pride. Each one is a unique example, an incredible person to be admired. Their weaknesses are nothing but a decoration that puts the last touches on them; their defects, virtues concealed that push them to grow, and their talents, ah, their talents! These grow graced simply by my presence at their side! Because I believe in them with such force, that only the best emerges freely and abundantly. And it's that I, too, am better when beside my friends. They thrive in the positive, destroy darkness with their presence, and spread light with their wit, destroying the worst with a strike of exceptional humor. Vital, sarcastic, profound, funny, sensible or a bit crazy, only they know how to restore importance to all the heavy things in my life, those things that seem important but are really only urgent.

Friends light up our lives, reminding us that although we have forgotten how to play, with them we will know how to find the return road and become children once again. At their side, while we laugh, we calm the bull charges of life, redistributing the tensions that torment us, awakening from the day to day stuns, and we remember that life is also joy and fluidity.

Friends are the greatest blessing in the life of a person, and what a pity for the one who can't count them, though with the fingers of only one hand! Because true friends are rare, and it is true that every day it is more difficult to make a new good friend. But life has been generous with me and I continue having the fortune of increasing this unique and precious treasure with new incorporations into that kind of rare club of which I am the only manager. Being a member gives one the right to few things, but all of them undying: my unquestionable loyalty, my support, respect, advice (if they ask for it!), warmth, and attention in no greater measure than that of my own efforts, or what is even better, of the tandem that we create uniting the best of both of us.

In this pressed, devious, self-seeking, contemptible world where vile selfishness wanders around seeking its privileges like a king of the everyday, a group of people challenge its power with the invincible warmth of friendship, and they are my friends. Though I live one hundred years, I could never offer them enough gratefulness for existing. Pity on the ones who don't know what I am talking about! Let the world stop so they can get off. Life without friendship isn't worth being lived.

IN THE EYE OF THE HURRICANE

"To fly fast you must fold up the wings."
Juan Salvador Gaviota. Richard Bach

With the passing of the years, people clearly distinguish stages. In its simplest expression we remember "bad" times, we enjoy the "good" times. Some years are even like the Queen of England described, true "annus horribilis". Other times, less often, are those that we casually and easily forget, periods in which everything goes well, times of "wine and roses". In the eye of a hurricane, the winds are also light and the sky blue...

Pain, loss, unease, confusion, discouragement... the list is unending. Are so many things "bad"? So few things good?

The memory is an essential weapon for the consciousness of being and yet we know very little about it. We choose the things that we want to remember, but this process continues being a mystery to a large extent. What is our first memory? No one knows how to answer this with certainty since the notion of time is not a variable that fits in well with memory. The brightest researches have already perceived the intense relationship that exists between memory and emotion. However, we continue to fix on details apparently unconnected with the event, particulars totally irrelevant that are able to take on importance while we forget essential things or what we consider transcendental. One of the memory's weapons in its connection with emotions is forgetfulness. We manage to forget things that we never believed could disappear from our mind while we were living them. However, the bad moments stay well imprinted in the memory, and to the point where we can make a calendar of our lives based on this type of memory. Physical pain marks moments, but it is undoubtedly emotional pain that leaves, in fire and blood, an indelible mark in our memory.

It is in difficult times that one measures the courage of the warrior. To the fine dining, the smile, the celebration, we all sign up in a hurry. It is in times of great turbulence when we prepare our true personal changes. And what happens is that the only positive meaning from these experiences resides in our capacity to learn from them, to question ourselves, and as a consequence, get over our deficiencies. They serve to confirm our virtues, to remember our true internal nature, our purpose in this life, and in this way they collaborate with the great purpose of forcing us to stay on course toward the port that we really want to get to.

In the face of difficulties, there are two options, to sink beneath the weight of the events, or grow from them. However, there are nuances that mustn't be left aside when it comes time to evaluate these two options.

To sink beneath the weight of the difficulties is not a positive option, although as Martial Artists we know the saying: To sink beneath the weight of the snow is a sign of a wise attitude. It is evident that the idea of the saying is not to surrender, but to gently yield, reconsider, adapt, these are its positive points. If we resist change and remain rigid and inflexible, we can break. However, a minimum and indispensable "positive opposing tension" must be maintained so that the snow doesn't break the branch. The strategy? Wait, resist, persevere in the positive, crouch into our tight position, and lie in wait for the right moment to counterattack. It is then when one has to "grow" in the face of difficulty, open the wings and take off flying higher than we ever have before. Fighting things stubbornly and aggressively only expands one's structure, offering more surface over which more weight is gathered and generated.

Problems bring us down, they force us to lose confidence, and this is a natural response under their weight; however, we mustn't allow them to leave us cold, frightened or depressed. In confronting this pressure we must maintain that positive tension that the bamboo leaf exercises; a tension "without tension" that arises from a flexible attitude in order to reconsider, in order to change; a firm attitude to keep the force alive, although under the cold weight of the snow.

As Juan Salvador Gaviota said, "To fly fast you must fold the wings." Offering less resistance to the winds of life allows us to pass lightly between the storm clouds, less exposed to the caprices of the winds of change, to the bolts of the unexpected. If when you fly the sun shines and everything is apparently calm, be suspecting of the worst like Ulysses, for you are in the eye of the hurricane.

THE SUPREME TEACHING OF COMBAT

"The one who does something has everyone against him: those who do the same, those who do the opposite, and those who do nothing."

Let there be no doubt in anyone's mind, combat is the very essence of Martial Arts, its first and last reason for existing. However, the confrontation with another individual, with an opponent, is only a weak imitation of the true combat of the warrior, the combat with oneself.

After a certain point along the path of individual learning, there is only one way to progress, measuring oneself with the world. In this way, fighting is not a part of the whole of what a student must learn, but the concrete expression of that which he or she studies. Confronting an opponent puts to the test not only your technical level, but also and especially your self-control and your evolutionary level.

Aggression has a specific function in the protection of the self, however, this is generally perceived by our society as an unwelcome and unhealthy way. Violence and aggression have become a synonym of "bad". This shouldn't sound odd to anyone, since the group fears what stands out, what breaks the norms or the balance, what produces uncertainty, what instigates any kind of action aimed at making things more dynamic and living it as another way of questioning the established order. Even in the case of the individuals being subjected to unpleasant situations, tyrannies full of horrors for everyone and, on paper, unacceptable, the society—those groups of gregarious animals that we humans are—doesn't in any way sympathize with those making use of their ability to undertake actions that call that society into question. However, these same groups of people can possibly, pushed on by a strong leadership, be capable of unleashing the furies and open Pandora's box . There are many examples of both reactions in the history of mankind, reactions, in both cases, able to surprise and upset those who want to judge them from our current vision of the world. It is certain, in any case, that in times of "peace" and in modern societies, aggression as a force and manifestation of human nature tends to be inhibited and repressed. Our bodies suffer that repressing tension and manifest it in the traces that said attitude leaves on our bodies and faces.

Frowns, tense shoulders, closed hands, rigidity, and, of course, tense jaws that scrape and grind the teeth at night, expressing its aggression at the only time that the consciousness lets it... a fashionable disease at its peak, you only have to ask a dentist friend!

Martial Arts are a positive way to channel, to re-discover yourself, and enjoy that present from nature, capable of helping any person on his path toward his or her essential being, toward that squashed and repressed part of ourselves, toward that space where the animal that we carry inside cries out to be heard, integrated, and accepted in our whole being. And it is in combat when the neophyte comes face to face with this particular dispossession of himself, so blocked and negated that he doesn't know how to confront it. There are two reactions, which those who have been involved in this for some time know.

1) The highly inhibited person is incapable of shouting, carrying out techniques, they get tense protecting themselves any way they can and possibly outlines some technique or something similar to what is studied in classes, but he or she does it simply to get out of the predicament and follow along with the circumstances, doing what he or she believes is expected in a bad, uncoordinated way. This pale and rigid person sweats copiously in a cold sweat, showing intense interior congestion. Of course, one day it explodes and the Master must be attentive in order to make sure that the secondary effects of this process don't hurt others or the person himself.

2) The person has no control, openly shows his or her aggression in an irate manner and not considerate toward learning companions; he or she outlines techniques that in some way have been studied; they get confused, they shout continuously, they get red, and try to inhibit their opponent advancing in a sloppy and unbalanced way towards him, but his shouts only manifest his own fear instead of his interior force, his vertigo in the face of the emptiness in which he finds himself, his desperation at knowing himself, in spite of everything, as tremendously vulnerable, and his anger facing his inability to put order to a chaotic situation that drives him towards quick exhaustion.

For the expert, combat is something very different. A combat is an opportunity to measure oneself against another, but especially to enjoy measuring oneself against oneself. For the expert, the opponent is a complete unknown that must be deciphered, possessor of his strong points where he should be avoided, holder of weak points that must be discovered and attacked. The opponent, not necessarily an enemy, is a mirror in which one looks at oneself. His strikes will undoubtedly show us our weakest points; he, like us, will try to take advantage of any tiny bit of indecision, of any weakness in our guard, of any signs of stupidity, of any lack of synchrony in our whole Being.

In the end, it's that combat, once the technical aspects are superseded, realizes itself in the measure of two spirits confronting one another. All of the great ones in this matter have spoken about this. Musashi, Sun Tzu, and so many others describe for us the courage of the warrior as an essential tool to reach that singular mental, physical, and spiritual state that we observe in the great Masters. Such a state has been expressed repeatedly with phrases like "the absolute emptiness". That includes the total release of any mundane matter, the most complete and inhuman sensation that nothing, absolutely nothing, is important; not even victory, not even defeat, reducing everything to the immediate, free, and fluid experience of the here and now. Only from that emptiness is the expert able to anticipate his opponent, reducing the effectiveness of any action he is going to undertake, even before he is capable of unleashing it, even managing to return it against him and in this way resolving his duel with a proportional and restrained gesture that neutralizes his opponent with the minimum effort and the maximum efficiency.

Whoever has, at some time, even fleetingly, felt or discerned the power inherent in that state, knows that nothing equals it and that that was the reason of all those years chasing the mastery of combat with untiring force. Only when we are able to flow calmly in the clamor of battle can we say that we have learned what combat has to teach us. To beat many is only a sign of technical skill, but to beat oneself, just like the Tao Te Ching states, is the sign of wisdom.

POLITICALLY CORRECT

"Only those who take calmly what keeps
the people of the world occupied
can take care of the things that
the people of the world take calmly."
Chang Chao

There are things that one cannot say and even less write these days.

A new kind of censorship, imposed like all of them by the mediocre, is opening right and left in the West: the "politically correct".

Pushed in most cases by the Universal Law of the pendulum, the "description of the world" of the societies—in other words, their idea of good and bad, of what is excellent and what is disastrous—is changing, and as has always occurred, with the help and the acquiescence of the most ignorant, those who believe what is said for one reason only... because many people repeat it. The new priests of modern society (now they wear white robes or neckties!) elaborate their reports, their proclamations, and their decrees, amplifying them by the complacent mass media that rarely dares to question their "sacred word". The result? An enormous stultifying of the neurons, and the continuous bleating of sheep, repeating the same lies that on many occasions reach the grotesque.

Examples? Might I give examples without being burned at the stake of the heretics? Surely not, if I questioned things like positive discrimination (Is it possible for discrimination to be positive?), the anti-tobacco laws, the idea that Martial Arts are violent, and so many other things that would be best not to even mention! For that, in no way would I do it in a public platform (if that was how I thought), since the only thing that I would achieve with such a treacherous and unbeneficial attitude would be to create a scandal, and of course, suffer the anathema of those who speak ex catedra, condemning me to listen to arguments full of folly, but yes, repeated to satiation! And what is worse, things already accepted as universal truth and untouchable, in fact, converted into common ground, unquestionable dogma, accepted by all, questioned by none.

The established always appears before us as something rocky; it has been forming with the sediments of change, with the sedimentation of events, with the passing of many lives. We imagine the established as irremovable since that is how it seems to us today, but for that very reason we know with absolute sureness that it won't be here tomorrow. If there is anything permanent in and of itself, it is change, and given that everything responds to the Universal Law of the pendulum, to the laws of opposition and complements, the cyclic laws... definitively, to the always changing infinite movement of the Tao, it would be magnificent to be able to openly speculate about all of that which calls into question the things that everyone accepts at the same time and as certain these days. Human beings strive to improve on the work of nature and often we don't realize that we always achieve the exact opposite of what we try. We fight against bacteria with antibiotics... we make them stronger and ourselves weaker... we want to cool the air in our homes and raise the exterior temperature with our air-conditioners; we condemn violence as bad, we want to contain it, but it always returns changed and increased, etc., etc.

However, not all of us can keep quiet facing this show, perhaps imbued with some Promethian spark, perhaps pushed by hatred of stupidity, perhaps... simply to take the contrary position. In the end, we live in the times that were handed to us, we are the protagonists of this moment right now in human evolution and in some way we feel that we belong to the tribe, and in our way we love it with all its defects, and perhaps even because of them!

There are good ways and bad ways to manage chaos, but idiots are not among my favorites. I have never liked the bonfires that burn ideas, books, or people... I admit that prohibitions bother me, but this must be a remnant of the rebel in me. I believe that to create a limit is the best way to encourage someone to go past it, but that doesn't mean I don't understand restraint, the need to manage order, and among these ways, I always prefer those that do it by channelling the forces of the events instead of using the forces to suppress. I am much more inclined toward intelligent methods, those that consider the defects of its creators, giving a margin of action in its application in order to be able to adapt; I prefer the firm but flexible since I irremediably love that marvellous and most important of human sense, common sense (that which is the least common of the senses!). I love to discover it applied with that emotional and pragmatic intelligence that knows no limits of reason, and for that teaches one to apply creativity to all ideas, generosity to all conclusions in a magnanimous and even friendly and gentile way.

There are many things that I don't believe, many opinions that I don't share, truths proclaimed to the four winds, aired by "authorized" voices, but lacking authority, those who want to impose what are no more than fleeting opinions as universal truths. How are grandchildren are going to laugh at us when they read what we had to say about health, science, society, etc.! Perhaps they will judge us just like we judge today those who burned Galileo at the stake for affirming that it was the earth that rotated around the sun and not the other way around, like those who decided to allowed the Blacks to be slaves because, unlike the docile natives, they didn't have a soul…

I don't believe that evolution is a slow process, the fruit of the passing of time. I believe that it is more that it goes in qualitative leaps. I think that these are not casual rather the fruit of the courage and talent of people who knew, people who dared to question the accepted, the established. There have always been those responsible for the changes in our idle, lazy species. Precisely those who all the others invariably wanted to hang by their thumbs, crucify or silence in the bonfire.

Perhaps now it is not necessary to destroy so clearly these dissident and disobedient voices; maybe the background noise is such that we can't even hear the voices! Perhaps stupidity has reached the point to where no one can even think of having a different look, and furthermore, there is the "politically correct".

Meanwhile, Inquisition-minded ones, if you act with "good will", allow me to remind you of that refrain that says, "God frees us from good intentions"; if what you proclaim is that it is you who are the safeguards of humanity, there are others who affirm, "God frees us of our friends, the enemies I take care of myself"; and if what they want to make me believe is that they hold absolute truth, I can't help but remember that other one who affirms, "there is no good idiot".

No. Today I will not be politically incorrect; as someone much more important than I once said: "He who has eyes to see, let him see. He who has ears to hear, let him hear."

"Human beings strive to
improve on the work of
nature and often we don't
realize that we always
achieve the exact opposite of
what we try"

JIMMY: BORN AN ARISTOCRAT, DIED A WARRIOR

"Don't hope to find a secret technique, rather perfect your mind with continuous training, that is the key to victory."
Kyuzo Mifune

It was a precious cinnamon-colored poodle. Since its birth, in a good house, it grew up spoiled and pampered, very well taken care of. As soon as it was weaned, it left to live with my aunt Lala in the Tucci family house, on Lavalle Street in Buenos Aires. Lala had a maternal spirit after spending many years helping to bring up her 9 little brothers and sisters, and she found in Jimmy the perfect object for her warm attention and caring.

Jimmy grew up eating like a prince: rich roasted leftovers, corn cakes, delicious pastries, fatty sweets, and so on. As is natural, this delicious and abundant food wound up undermining its health. One bad day, Jimmy's natural joy succumbed to the saturation of good food. They immediately called the best veterinarian in the city. The doctor auscultated, frowned, and finally proclaimed his verdict: "fatty liver; sugar; diet is indispensable." From then on, Jimmy, always attended to with care, ate his rice soup and grated apples—that, yes!—in the moment so that they didn't oxidize.

Jimmy was, without a doubt, a peculiar dog and especially intelligent. The care and good education he had received made him another member of the family. Back then, the one writing this was just a little, restless baby, but Jimmy understood quickly that I was part of his pack. Each time I appeared at the house, Jimmy stuck to me, followed me around, and took care of me. On one occasion, the poodle prevented a nest of caterpillars from falling into my crib while I slept under a tree in the family's country house. Among all the anecdotes, the most incredible occurred while I was taking a nap in an adjoining bedroom where the older people got together. Jimmy, as always, stayed by my side, but not without first listening to the firm recommendations of its owner, who he seemed to understand perfectly. A short time after leaving us alone, Jimmy began to whine mournfully, but since no one paid any attention, the tone increased little by little until my mother and aunt Lala came into the room.

The scene was tremendous: Jimmy, with his back raised and against the bed, supported the baby who, having moved around while sleeping, had gotten dangerously close to the edge of the twin bed. The dog was uncomfortable and whined, but lowly so as not to wake me. On that occasion, without me yet conscious, a special relationship began between myself and our canine friends, a relationship that some of my reader friends already know perfectly well.

One day, my aunt Lala had to leave Buenos Aires for a week, so she left her dog in the charge of my uncle Babo, an active colonel at that time, who took the dog out for a walk in the Forests of Palermo Park. They took long walks in which the reborn Jimmy ran around and improved his health. It was on one of those walks when Jimmy, until then always attentive to calls, mysteriously disappeared. Missing, my uncle didn't stop searching for him until night fell, but it was all in vain. Jimmy, that little dog, couldn't survive, everyone said, that most spoiled of dogs!

For a whole week, my uncle the colonel mobilized an entire regiment to look for his sister's dog. The soldiers searched the forests day and night and each day the anxiety of my poor uncle grew. Babo, whose real name was Eduardo Anibal, resembling his homonym, general Cartagines, distressingly directed his army on foot and on horse instead of elephants, covering the enormous park that gives life to the beautiful city of Buenos Aires. How would he be able to tell his sister that Jimmy was lost? However, all his efforts were useless and finally he had to assume that Jimmy had disappeared.

The forest rangers of Palermo, who with so much coming and going had come to know my uncle perfectly, told him months later that they had seen Jimmy on various occasions. The cinnamon-colored poodle was the chief of the wild dogs that lived in large and savage packs. The rangers tried again and again to get him, but there was no way. Jimmy, always more astute, found a way to outwit them and continue his days as the chief of the dogs in the Forests of Palermo.

My aunt had more poodles and all of them were called Jimmy, but there was only one real Jimmy.

From this story, a fable but not invented, we can all learn something. Jimmy, the paradigm of the intelligent and friendly dog, came to be a fierce leader capable of bringing in line dogs that were much bigger than him, and all of that after living a life of comfort! In the end, he demonstrated having the necessary resources to bring out the wolf in him.

There are those who confuse the gentleness of the strong, the warmth and the openness of one who, having been brought up with love, knows how to confide in life, with weakness of character. There are those who think that the one who doesn't want to fight only acts out of cowardice.

Magnanimity has always been the privilege of the great spirits, only the weak, in their lack of confidence, can't understand it; like a dog beaten and abandoned, will growl and show its teeth while in reality and at the same time, it has its tail between its legs. To the weak, anxiety and fear make them aggressive, and it is this same aggression that condemns them to receive painful responses to their inadequate behavior more and more frequently; in this way, entering into a vicious circle of terror, they won't stop reaping what they sow. One can't always justify this blind rage by blaming "others" for our own miseries, rather it is better to take responsibility of our lives. Breaking the chain of self-inflicted pain... is there a more urgent task?

Confusing generosity and gentleness with weakness or frailty is a common error among those driven by their insecurity, they expose themselves by attacking others systematically, without even having calmed themselves. Malorum causae if they aren't able to discriminate! Perhaps, behind the sweet poodle there is really a fierce wolf hidden within.

MARTIAL CINEMA HAS DIED, LONG LIVE MARTIAL CINEMA!

"That all life is a dream, and dreams are dreams".
Luis Eduardo Aute quoting Calderón de la Barca

Agreat friend of mine, a film buff all his life, a great defender of the seventh Art who loves to watch and talk about films of the past, surprised me the other day with an affirmation: "They don't make films anymore, now they just shoot long video clips."

I don't want to succumb to that "any time in the past was better", but it is true that the "dream factories" of past times have now become an ongoing storefront window of the computer industry and its advances. Special effects, simply a resource in the past, are today the most important element of a film and the area where Cinema in the past decades has concentrated its efforts to evolve and change.

It doesn't surprise me; I find it a paradigmatic symptom of our times, times in which the substance of things has yielded its place to form. Given that the world of Cinema is wholly phantasmagorical and "Neptunian" (lights and shadows projected on a wall like in the myth of Plato's cave), it is logical that in it these tendencies that are already quite noticeable in other areas are expressed to the extremes. The script is not as important as before, the re-makes multiply (And now King Kong 3 or 4?); the ideas seem to have been exhausted, which can be noticed when what you receive arrives as "sensor-round and pixels", a way of submitting ourselves to a chair for a treatment more fitting of "A Clockwork Orange" than of a film session. Given that there are no ideas, they raise the volume (that comes out from who knows where!), they submit you to a third degree capable of saturating all your senses (there are even films with odors!) with the objective of making you "feel something". Instead of making the soul vibrate, the emphasis is on filling the senses to the brim, deep emotion has been substituted by banal sentimentalism, and thinking... well... about that the least said the better, as you know. Cinema, generally speaking, is one more consumer product. It isn't that it wasn't before—never has an Art been more connected to money than this one—but there was room for dissent, creativity and emotion. Great geniuses of the screen reeled off a thousand and one surprises, they captivated us with their fascinating stories (in which, by the way, you didn't know what was going to happen!), they made us dream, laugh, and cry.

One of the consequences of this situation in Cinema in general has supposed, unsuspectingly only a few years ago, an unexpected advantage for our sector. The bag of ideas completely empty, Cinema has begun to swallow itself up, whether with the recourse that I have mentioned of the re-makes and the series (Star Wars 39?) or with exploring the genres that before were considered secondary, which is the case of Martial Arts films. Said reaction has brought lights and shadows to our genre, but what can't be doubted is that it has reached audience levels that were unthinkable some years ago.

Ang Lee (Tiger and Dragon), Jhon Woo, and, of course, Quentin Tarantino, have taken the genre to the forefront of audience levels with a manifest love of the action films of the past. Tarantino's winks at Bruce Lee are a continuous game in which the costumes, takes, and scenery bring us back in a continuous homage to a phenomenon that began as cult films and wound up becoming a genre in and of itself.

"Matrix", the maximum exponent of the Cinema of effects, and which has undoubtedly established a before and after for action film, has maintained in its script, beyond fights and effects, the essences of a world of knowledge closely related to the road of the warrior in martial traditions. It is true that with it died the martial actors as such (anyone trained a few months and suspended from cables is capable of doing on screen what Bruce Lee never even dared to dream about!), but it is no less certain that the discourse, created around a world of symbols and established on the myths of tradition, has taken to the public the essences of what is Martial as a way of initiation (the world of knowledge beyond the apparent), and it has done so with great success, in a rotund, intense way, like an overdose, which has soaked into—and how!—the collective unconscious of modern societies.

The "Matrix" phenomenon has opened Pandora's Box, the myths of always, today recycled in series like "The Lord of the Rings" that make their appearance in the market pushed by the lack of ideas with substance and novelty.

Today we turn our eyes back to pay homage and review that Martial Arts cinema which today feeds the revolution that Tarantino, Matrix, and the Lord of the Rings have brought to a zenith. Cinema in which the protagonists really knew how to fight, when they were accomplished Martial Artists, and from out of which came geniuses like Bruce Lee, capable of revolutionizing the Martial panorama beyond their skills as actors. If you can make Thurman kick as if she were Bill Wallace, of what value are stunt specialists?

Martial Cinema as we have known it, dominated by the great screen names, true martial artists, have died these days, sublimated to a technological caricature of themselves. They say that the end of the cycles is the most flavourful, the seed is always contained within the fruit, and we have to ask ourselves, nonetheless, what will come. Jackie, the eternal Jackie, is producing the best of himself in his latest films, distinguished by unquestionable personal values and by knowing how to surf the big wave of special effects, without further recourse than that of his congeniality and doing a good job, but no new names are coming out. Seagal has been doing nothing exciting in the past years and in each new film, his followers await what never arrives... Van Damme, who seems to have overcome his problems, reappears on the screens that saw better times for him. Bruce, of course, left us and that's that.... Chuck Norris continues being impeccable as a Texas Ranger and it seems that if he decided to cancel the series it wasn't for a lack of audience rather for the logical fatigue of doing more of the same... and the years go on for everyone, and "Charlie" has already done it all.

Jet Li goes here and there delivering notable strikes, younger than the rest, and even has his own video game, and we are sure that he will give us some more jewels if the producers know how to get out what he has within. Shwazzenegger is governor of California (future president?). The cult of the body that "Conan the Barbarian" established has never had a more relevant echo, and it's that Shwazzenegger knew how to build a career in which he intelligently did not demark himself along one line, providing us with comedies of unquestionable good taste and success but that are no longer—by any means—in the realm of action films. However, the governor, a big fan of health, sports, and, of course, body building, has supported the Martial Arts and continuous organizing one of the most important fairs in the sector in the USA under his name.

The intrinsic values of martial Cinema have been incorporated into general Cinema. Action films (of late, Hollywood produces few without this ingredient) gave the fan a space where he or she could enjoy the combat scenes that were later analyzed with valor and passion. People like Rorion Gracie contributed their bit of realism in the films of Mel Gibson as a crazed policeman, and the cameos of Benny, Jet, and even Dan Inosanto have always been very celebrated by the lovers of the sector. But beyond the fights, Martial Cinema has known how to touch that hunger for a hero that lies behind the public, formed by the collective of practitioners of the disciplinary Arts. For this reason, films like Star Wars with images of combats done with "luminous katanas" or the magnificent battles of Lord of the Rings or of The Last Samurai have conquered our sector, not only for the fights, not only for the theme with their Eastern pop-eye, but also, and especially, for their focus, more or less on the models of the warrior, on the hero who defends a dignified and always difficult way of acting, and who is able to defend with his sword. That warrior ethic is loved by those who enjoy that archetypical image beyond the forms and knows how to seduce the spectator who in the past connected with Gary Cooper in "High Noon". What doubt is there that the settings of The Last Samurai are also an added component so that all lovers of the Japanese traditions, in particular, and Eastern traditions, in general, have an added enjoyment that is never overdone.

It is an entire genre, that of Martial films, that is indebted to some of the names that we analyze in this publication especially dedicated to the many, many fans of a genre that paradoxically at the height of its glory, disappears at the end of its splendid trajectory like a river that sinks into the sea of modern cinema, and to which it has essentially contributed in the past decades. The times are gone in which the actor had to be a martial artist, and where the fact of being very gifted and an expert martial artist formed a significant part of the success.

The king of the genre, Bruce Lee, and his court of distinguished colleagues remain in everyone's memories, an indispensable and just reference to an epoch that is already leaving. The roads of the future are other, undoubtedly different, but no less hopeful; roads on which the hearts of the lovers of the genre will have to find the satisfaction of their desires in productions that can't be categorized in our genre, but sufficiently "contaminated" by that special thing, which perhaps cannot be seen as a differential fact, but that undoubtedly contributes aromas of that always indecipherable and ennobler of the human spirit that is the shadow of the warrior spirit.

I am sure that you will enjoy this project, a collectible that closes an unrepeatable era worthy of our homage.

FOR MEN ONLY...

"The education of a child is the responsibility of the whole tribe."
African Saying

Probably in these times, the very energy of the planet and the bands that it crosses on its trip through the cosmos require it to be so, but there is no doubt that the masculine is badly seen, its time almost up, and consequently the consciousness of the group puts everything that smells of it in a corner.

The masculine is quite scarce in the Universe. Compared to the great Yin of the astronomical space, there are only little bits of Yang, light that is barely visible in the immensity of the vast emptiness. The masculine, active, condensed, alight, etc. is the exception in the face of the great entropy; life and consciousness are something even less frequent.

I know that some will immediately try to argue that said categorizations are an atavistic remains, the fruit of a "chauvinistic" and "oppressive" culture, and they will wonder why, and on what grounds, we decided that Yang is masculine and corresponds to the luminous. It could be explained from various angles, philosophical, astronomical, and especially physical; it could be noted how this knowledge is analogous in all the traditional cultures on the planet, but such an effort is worthy of another editorial, or even an entire book, though a book that I'm not thinking of writing because it is already written; I edited it some years ago and if it is only available in Spanish, it is worthy of the attention of all those who really want to understand something about the laws of polarity in the Universe, about Yin and Yang. (Universo Polar, Eyras, Jose Maria Sanchez Barrio).

In our societies, the feminine clearly imposes itself, and in such a way that all masculine aspects are considered negative, to the point that men themselves, the few that are left, almost have to apologize, or better yet, shut up before openly exposing our opinions and "feelings". Like a new social plague, more and more groups of men communicate with themselves in a low voice while they look out of the corners of their eyes before openly sharing their points of view with their colleagues not to be hung in a public square for ridicule along with others who dare to give an opinion on what they are.

When I write this, I'm not trying to be impartial, nor comprehensive, nor show solidarity; those are feminine values. I am trying to write like I am and my objective in doing so is not to engage in a fiery speech or hide behind the group in order to defend my postulates; I do it to exercise my freedom and encourage my equals to do the same, although the means is absolutely hostile. If we don't do it this way, not only will the lice eat us, but furthermore, our children will turn out handicapped. I do it especially to open the eyes to the new generations that haven't had the opportunity to see things except from one pole, with all the vices that such a focus carries with it, and all the destructive consequences that we are observing.

I believe that education is a great key that opens many doors. If it is biased or slanted, it is the work of all conscious beings to act as a scale, pointing out such imbalances. As the African saying goes: "The education of a child is the responsibility of the whole tribe."

Mars is a masculine god and the Arts of Mars (as much as I prefer the goddess Minerva as an example of what we do!) are from Mars, and therefore masculine. For that reason I understand that their practice and teaching can act as a counterweight in an education based essentially on feminine values. It seems to me that this is in and of itself already a great contribution to the group, but we mustn't in any way reject our capacity to influence other spheres, like those relative to thought, even if that can be worse than navigating against the current knowing that a little way down the river turns into a waterfall.

I am not in any way proposing to yield to the temptation (and that with all that tightens!) of an absurd return to the past or making bad postulates of a particularly chauvinist slant; to be masculine doesn't mean being sexist, though, of course, it does mean being a male, that said without asperity—rather the opposite—toward the females.

The past is only a touching stone, a rung that allows us to climb up the

ladder of evolution and consciousness, a point of support in order to go further. Abstain from the nostalgic notions of attributing to my words any support of their postulates. However, to try to ignore the biological basis that has step by step through millions of years established man as he is and woman as she is an enormous stupidity, a stupidity into which, day after day, I see the spokespeople of our civilization in the media fall. Probably this is one of the most obvious results of the abuse and bringing down of the masculine that our civilization is committed to. The loss of the polarity isn't an advantage to anyone, though those who look at it short-sightedly or in a biased mentality might think so. The strength of the human being as a species arises from the tension between the sexes, lowering this differential is in all ways a catastrophe for our perpetuation, and a disaster for the individuals who live those times. The reason is simple: not knowing what one is and what are the essential orders that nature has given one as a victory, an inheritance from natural selection from our ancestors, will not bring us the peace or liberty that these voices called "revolutionary" or "liberating" promise, only frustration, lack of focus and balance, contradiction, and therefore confusion.

To verify that state of things, simply do a little survey and ask yourself, and consult your friends what answer they would give to the simple question: What does it mean to be a man? Or, what does it mean to you to be a woman?

All definitions are made marking the limits as well as describing the nature of the defined. If one replies honestly to these questions, one discovers that there is no recourse but to circumscribe the essential, the biological, to later attend to the functional. My friends, it's their call, if they listen to their conclusions, almost for sure all of them will sound very bad to the ears of the politically correct… almost assuredly.

As I have already filled this page, I have no choice but to leave you with this diatribe so that you can wrestle with it during the month, lacking sufficient space to declare my point of view. But no, don't feel alone! I won't abandon you to such a task. I promise to return next month to dot the i's of that concerning the differences derived from biology and give them a hand (if that's what they need!) to continue thinking together in the way we are and freely.

Meanwhile, be careful! In these themes, being a man and saying what one thinks can cause problems for you… They are going to have to put a note on us like tobacco! "BEING A MAN CAN CAUSE UNPLEASANTRIES" In such a situation, going out into the street without a helmet is bold. So take care! There are less and less of us!

TO BE A MAN IS TO BE A WARRIOR

To be a man at this time in history is a complicated matter, but that doesn't mean we should complain about it, since being a woman is, looking at the events, even more difficult. The depolarization is perhaps the marker that stands out the most at this time on the planet and I'm still amazed how the scientists ignore it. That tendency is only comparable to that of radicalization, whose effects are made clear all over the place, from world climate to the ideological level. We have gotten into a big mess as a species, but that mustn't cause us to leave aside dealing with the matters closer at hand, and what is closer at hand than our own natures!

One of these issues undoubtedly comes from the incredible distance that we have created between our biology and social questions. The abstract concept of equality, an essentially feminine concept, is imposed in such a way that it makes us forget what is evident and that is that men and women are not equal. You don't have to be a genius to notice!

The biology of man is like that of women, the result of millions of years of evolution and specialization. The brain of man is a magnificent structure, a computing center dedicated to tasks where concentration on a single matter outweighs that of dispersion. That happened as a result of the work of the hunter to which man dedicated himself, the fruit of his better physical disposition for intense effort, being taller, stronger, with a bigger liver, capable of a faster metabolism to feed the muscles, and a whole string of hormones that are abundant in him.

The hunter must concentrate on prey in order to be successful, while the collector must be able to discern the environment all around in order to find the berries among the branches in the forest. The feminine brain is an incredible mechanism of peripheral perception. This happened to the extent that those who were better fitted for these tasks were much more successful than those who didn't possess said capabilities and for that they reproduced, imposing their characteristics.

The structures of these brains resulted in absolutely different functions, as we have seen, and of course complimentary in regard to the work that they had. Biology evolves much slower than cultural guidelines, which can change in mere decades (or in hours if we take an airplane!). In the cultures of the industrialized nations, the guidelines for conduct have been distanced so far from biology that they have wound up provoking contradictions to such an extent that the result is personal disaster for millions of beings, lost in the chaos of evolution. For men, this jump supposes the cornering of his nature and the abdication of his talents and most elemental instincts. But the contradictions are time-bombs that always wind up exploding and the shock wave from such an explosion is watering the world with energetic cadavers, which in turn winds up denying his nature that is subjected to the surroundings.

Things are no better for the females of the species, taking on functions, behavior and even ideologies that crash head on with their natural instincts, looking for "men's freedom" instead of "finding" what undoubtedly lives within their nature.

The identity crisis had to have begun with the success of agriculture and the abandoning of nomadic groups dedicated to hunting and collecting. From a lunar and hunting cultural it changed to a solar and agricultural culture. The Sun was the new god and on it the crops depended, while the Moon marked the hunters' time, since its light supported the hunting parties and allowed for the chase that frequently lasted longer than a day. Stonehenge itself, according to the criteria of studies done on it, could be a Moon-Sun temple that the Druids built, the men of knowledge, in order to reconcile the rites of the old and the new era.

With agriculture, humans began to develop the sense of property and with it a much more defined fight for territory. The warrior ceased to be a hunter and man of knowledge in order to become more and more what we today know as military, that is, the one who manages violence, or the defense of the group territory, and later, that of the state. In the words of Sun Tzu: "Territory is the foundation of the state."

Socialization is a success of the feminine. The very society is essentially feminine. Men group together in order to have greater success in hunting, to learn and to share successful strategies, to later dance around the bonfire showing the scenes lived in the enactment of the celebration; afterward, once well-fed, they don't want to see the face of another man until the next hunting party, and with the stomach full, they prepare to dedicate themselves to the next important demand in their natures, a commandment, a vital command: "You will fertilize as many females as you can."

For that the presence of another man becomes very uncomfortable, for his interest in continuously meeting in fixed places is logically not a desire attributable to his nature.

However, for women, this was a magnificent opportunity to assert their greatest social talents. The ability to speak about anything and about various things at the same time (and understand oneself!) is a skill that continues to amaze men. This characteristic is trans-cultural, that is to say, it is not something singularly or exclusively ours: In Japanese, the kanjis to define the concept of "to speak" come from the image of three women around a well. In the exchange of information, physical force is not an essential pre-requisite; however, a brain equipped with a peripheral capacity can prosper in such circumstances. In the social game, women can assert their skills far more easily and choose among a greater number of males.

Furthermore, it is much easier to give birth and attend the babies in a stable population than one that is constantly moving.

The masculine, then, is not given precedence in the social context, although some insist that it is so. However, the distribution of tasks sought the way to accommodate the biological tendencies and every culture, in general, faced that dilemma through the symbolic substitution of functions. Instead of hunting game to fill the stomachs of the females and their offspring, man went out seeking a salary for sustenance. He had to be the provider, she the perpetuator of life. The roles did nothing but adapt themselves to a tendency established thousands of years ago when we walked around in leather skins in the forests of the planet trying to survive.

Culturally, we have changed a great deal, yet our biology has changed very little. The study of human remains from the first homo sapiens are not in essence distinct from what we are now. Taller, to be sure, perhaps only some characteristics are being imposed, the fruit of new, select values and parameters, for example, the hips of women tend to widen, we are losing the little toe, the wisdom teeth, etc., but our cranial capacity is essentially the same as that of our ancestors.

What does it mean to be a man in the XXI century?

Probably, as far as biology goes, there are very few differences, but in the cultural, an abyss. To re-discovering our essential masculine selves and accept it without prejudice is a good place to start in order to validate our daily life with our predatory and hunting nature. To try to establish moral categories and a priori, about what is good or bad in our tendencies through ideologies, religions, or moral positions is an enormous stupidity that will never get us in touch with our profoundest nature as a species, nor, of course, as a gender.

Aggression, that tendency marked by testosterone, so socially negative, must be re-channeled starting with its acceptance as a gift; in that, Martial Arts can offer us a great deal: the katas can be the substitute of those warrior dances where the bravery and the power of the warrior were a gift in the eyes of the tribe. The fights can be a kind of ritual of the confrontation with the enemy, and with other males for the females; training to strengthen the young people, to keep the race healthy and enrich the values of the spirit to confront the difficulties of life.

The only way to Be a Man today is to be a warrior and assume and integrate our past and in this way advance firmly toward the future. To deny our essential nature assuming the dictates and impositions of the cult of feminine values is more than to abdicate what we are, it is a castration without precedent to which we mustn't submit; only in this way will our essence be preserved and with it the necessary polarity, so that the big human tribe continues walking around the planet. Brave men together with firm and valiant women, Heaven and Earth that join in the mystery of life.

KATA!

The Japanese word KATA means form. The forms are very important in the Oriental tradition, in every sense, and its concept is very different from what we attribute to it in the West. Form is not etiquette, though it can be analogous to position, in the sense of arrangement, of posture. For the East, structure is what defines the function and the emphasis is therefore on the structural. The West has always been much more attentive to and focused on the functional. With us, it seems that we don't pay enough attention to the forms, to the arrangement, that is to say, to energetic structuring; rather, the West defines itself directly by the functional and its effects. For an Eastern strategist, the battle or a negotiation is won before it is fought, for a Westerner, the keys to battle are in the variables during its unfolding. The first gives priority to the arrangement of the forces, and the second to their mobility.

What is exceptional is that in these times of globalization, East and West, both sides of what is human (curiously coincidental with the functions of the cerebral hemispheres), have finally reached the same conclusion about the origin of matter. Science has done it through its studies in enormous particle accelerators; the East has achieved it through silence and calm. Such a conclusion is nothing more than that of matter arising continuously from emptiness, ordering itself in shapes.

But it is emptiness that really gives meaning to form. "The value of a cup is in its emptiness,"

the Zen tradition argues; "the spaces between the spokes are what gives function to the wheel," the Buddhists hold.

The forms, the Kata, are then something more than a collection of movements linked together with a precise energetic meaning, they are something more than a warrior dance that reproduces combat situations, and something more than a systemization of

pre-established movements with pedagogical intentions.

The forms have been designed to order the energy of the world moving the "fitting point", altering the consciousness of the practitioners.

This point is not a place defined on the body given that we are not dealing so much with a physical configuration, but like an energetic arrangement of our "luminous spheres". This concept, which can sound strange, makes reference to the sum of the potential energy that makes up a being. Today we know that matter is nothing more than organized energy. Everything in our Being, intellect, emotions, and physical body, is a form of energy vibrating in distinct ranges and tones that organizes itself like a sphere with luminous beams. The central focus from which these beams are coordinated, the critical point from which the central rotor of the Being executes its control and from which it is conscious of Being, is what is called "fitting point". To give evidence of its existence is one of the first objectives of all initiation into consciousness. The second step consists of learning to move it. The third step is to dominate that movement.

There are two kinds of forms: predominantly external forms, and those that are internal. The first primarily influence the technical and formal aspects of combat, the second the internalization, the making aware, and the energetic mobilization of the novice.

In the first, rapid movements, series, or the energy lines dominate, which conclude in an explosion known as Kiai, in which the shout marks the projection of energy; the second ones attend to breathing, are much less dynamic and lead the one executing it immediately to a change in his or her conscious state, a perceptible change even from the exterior by a sufficiently sensitive observer, even if they know nothing about the matter.

The internal Kata are generally considered superior forms and according to the Masters, they require a whole life of practice for their perfect execution. However, their powerful effects are felt immediately and their benefits can be enjoyed by any person who trains in it. It is certain that, as all powerful weapons, it has two edges and if one is not properly prepared, its effects can be disconcerting.

The forms have undergone adaptations and transformations through the years. If these are legitimate, then it is the Art that must adapt itself to the individual and not the contrary; many of them have been so radical that they have erased the initial effect for which they were designed. For that, the manuscript of the great-grandfather of Dr. Pereda handed down to us is a tool of great interest in order to re-discover some of the old forms of To-de, an original form which was later known as the Karate of Okinawa.

When a grand Master designs a form, he does it condensing his personal power into it in order to transform, in order to move the energies and to mobilize the consciousness of the one executing it in a precise direction. Its repetition offers an added value to the training.

Like the homeopathic medicines, the forms, when they have been well trained, act even in the simple process of preparing oneself for their execution. The forms re-structure the energy of the practitioner and lead him to an altered state of consciousness.

It is known that these days we can measure the vibratory values of our body in a precise way through its electric variables, among other ways. An expert acupuncturist or homeopath can define the state of an energy meridian in the body and apply the necessary doses for the patient, simply by putting him in contact with the medicine in the opposite hand with which he executes the measurement.

This occurs to the extent that each thing vibrates predominantly in one channel of energetic band, and this is no more than information that interacts with the organism, provoking a specific effect on it. In the same way, the Kata introduces information that forces all of our being to vibrate and organize itself energetically in accord with certain guidelines.

This transmutation is progressive and allows the student to continue discovering nuances in the same energetic tone, which, if it resounds in each one in a different way, they still have the same background melody. It is like two different wooden guitars playing the same tune.

Not long ago, the Grand Master Seikichi Uehara died, a man I had the privilege of meeting and who *Budo International* recorded an instructional video with when he was already an incredible 96 years old. In the interview that we had, he told me that he wanted to continue teaching the Art of his Master to 100, and he got it! He programmed his being in such a way that only three months after turning 100, he left this world. Such is the power that we can mobilize in our attempts, such is the power that creates our description of the world. In the end, what is real is only a perception and a changing state of consciousness.

To live to 100 is not an objective in and of itself, it is the way of living them that can make for an impassioned and transforming journey; first, of ourselves, and later, the environment.

Whether this is a positive transformation depends entirely and exclusively on us; those who hide behind the "It's just that..." and "But...", are undoubtedly very far from walking the way of the warrior.

THE "NEW" SELF-DEFENSE

"This we know: the earth doesn't belong to man; man belongs to the earth. This we know. Everything is connected, like blood that unites a family. Everything is connected."
- Letter from the Indian chief Noah Sealth to Franklin Pierce, president of the United States in the year 1854.

The presence of terrorism in Western societies is not new, but never has its influence marked a greater transformation of the paradigm of our way of life than nowadays.

The sharp hit delivered to the Western center of gravity that 9-11 supposed signals the end of the little remaining innocence on the civilian side of our societies facing a phenomenon that is now the object of analysis, and will be, for possibly a long time.

In the opinion of Dr. Lorenzo Castro, Phd in sociology and expert on terrorism: "This battle will last another 50 years." I wouldn't know whether to say my wise and respected friend, Dr. Castro—by nature not very optimistic—was being so or not on this occasion. His predictions (some of which came true 25 years ago already!), the confessions during those infinite youthful nights, (the majority of times in front of the priceless beers that relieved our "martial sweat"), have come to pass inexorably, in such a way that, seen from a distance, they seem more like the verdicts of a sorcerer than the opinions of a scientist. I wish he were wrong this time, but I wouldn't bet on it.

Another old friend of mine criticized our magazine on a certain occasion: "It's a very well done publication, but it's `out of sync' with the times; it doesn't treat the realities of the here and now of the planet." Apart from my never having agreed with this criticism (I must add that he didn't practice Martial Arts), I was never less in agreement than on this occasion when I am just about to write what is perhaps the most difficult editorial that I have ever faced.

At first, I decided to do this extra edition as a result of the natural evolution of the editorial line that the kind readers of the monthly editions of *Budo International* know well, a line that justly embraces law enforcement agents and soldiers as being parts intrinsically united to the very context of the "Arts of Mars". This inclusion (widely criticized at first by other magazines in the sector that have, nonetheless, wound up imitating us and by individual voices that don't like said philosophy) is being amply justified by the accumulation of unfortunate events that have been putting into question many things in our lives.

A new concept of "self-defense" is taking shape, an emergence pushed by the "very stubborn reality", a much broader concept that doesn't stop at the development of the necessary skills to disarm an opponent, win a championship, or avoid their stealing your wallet as in the old days. It is a concept that comes with heavy steps, forcing every citizen, whether martial artist or not, to remain in a permanent state of alert as part of his or her daily survival.

To those who think I am exaggerating, I invite you to spend any day of the week in the subway in the city of Madrid. No, it isn't only that every five minutes they tell you on the intercom that you shouldn't separate from your bags, nor leave a package or backpack even for a second. It is namely the effect that is provoked noticing those looks, those faces with which the citizens mutually keep an eye on each other. A new tension can be felt in the atmosphere; it is the hidden flame, the embers of the recent wound, but also, and especially, the fear, the terror, and the anxiety of all of us facing the certainty that it could happen again here and now.

In the subway in Madrid, people, the normal citizens, before relaxed and dozing off in that subterranean limbo on their way to their daily duties, are now vigilante goalkeepers, attentive agents of security, both their own security and that of others.

Everyone has cried for the ones who fell in the attacks, inconsolably in the case of the closest ones; for them, their friends and families, they are irreparably lost. But for the remaining social fabric, after the impact, life continues. The declarations of intentions by the politicians, the grandiloquent words, have already gone. What stops us from forgetting? The sentimentalist argument, saturated by the continuous media bombardment, doesn't have much power (as always!); people want—need—to get back to normal, to turn the page... one can go down into the depths, but one can't stay there too long, the pressure is unbearable and life inexorably continues.

However, a sentiment is produced, found paradoxically among the population: We don't want to hear about it anymore, we want to forget, continue on, take up our things where we left them... but there... there we can't return... things will never be like before; from now on, only one force imposes itself with sufficient power to avoid our acting like ostriches, the certainty that our old friend fear contributes.

The new concept of self-defense includes unheard-of knowledge, as much for the classic Martial Artist as for the normal citizen, which was before only the concern of a minority of experts and security and law enforcement agents. Knowledge and concepts that as a consequence can only be acquired from the hand of chosen specialists, such as those who I have invited to write in this edition, all of them, on the other hand, habitual authors of articles and columns in this medium and their illustrative compliments, the videos and DVDs. Their disposition and response to the project has been immediate. They, more than anybody, know how important it is for the greatest number of people possible to be made conscious and be prepared to be able to react positively facing the challenge that terrorism supposes to our present and future. This is a battle in which "citizen collaboration" must transform into something more than a kind of "civil military".

I want to add, esteemed readers, that about said authors, I can only give, and have only been able to give, limited information about their activities, duties, and responsibilities, but believe me when I tell you that each and every one of them is a person with proven experience; I don't want to miss the opportunity to thank them for their attentive response and support so that this extra edition can see the light. From different origins, countries, and even points of view, at times even opposing (with which this editorial doesn't necessarily have to agree), they are, nonetheless, united by the common denominator of being of a very high professional level. To all of them, my respect and graditude.

Yes, the self-defense of the XXI century includes indispensable knowledge in matters that we had never before posed as those directly concerning martial practices. From among all of them, I would like to highlight what I consider to be principal: intelligence.

Intelligence in the double sense: First, in that of developing our capacity to discern the hidden forces that underlie the events that we are living (and that we are going to live), in order to adopt an attitude of alertness and positive action facing the challenge presented by terrorism; and in order not to be manipulated by special interests, always hidden behind—and willing to take advantage of—each historical impulse. Definitively, intelligence to direct and capitalize on the great deal of information that comes to us each day concerning this phenomenon and in order to see further, reading between the lines and offering some light to a phenomenon, to a tremendously dark panorama. Darkness (Master Yoda remembers when Skywalker was going to enter the cave) cannot be fought effectively except in one way: turning lights on that dissipate it!

The second is the intelligence in the sense of the information services, who will have to learn how to permeate the terror networks, infiltrating agents, buying people, and doing everything necessary in the dark and Plutonian world of secret agents, and in this way, to be able to anticipate the enemy, cut off their sources, attack their plans, their allies, surround them, and finally reduce them to extinction. This is going to involve a lot of effort in which all of us are going to be in some way implicated. The old diatribe between freedom and security will prowl through our lives, but undoubtedly, winning this battle will require a lot more, like intense re-focusing, profound questioning that can't be delayed, and iron wills. The greatest force of democracy has always been its capacity to be influenced by, and its adaptability to, the changing circumstances of the winds of history. I'm sure that now is not the time when the level of such effort is going to be less than before.

The self-defense of the new Era forces us, Martial Artists, to put our knowledge at the service of society. Believe me. They themselves say so! Still, they are few; there are still a totally insufficient number of adequately prepared agents. From our experience in fighting with and without weapons, we can (and every day we are more and more!) contribute training and psycho-physical preparation formulas to these men who work under tremendous pressure, and badly paid, in the trenches, and in the new paradigm, this trench line can be on any street, airplane, subway, train, or bus in the West. For that, we should consider positive actions in order to act directly, such as, for example, to teach our students everything possible in reference to this new challenge since we are because of history, all part of this effort, all soldiers in this battle. This implies an additional effort of preparation by the Masters, an effort, you can be sure, which students will learn more and more how to value as a compliment to your classes, whatever style you practice. In the end, despite nobody liking it, everyone is conscious of this need, and if not now, they will be left with no other alternative than to accept it later. That's how ugly the situation is, friends!

From this philosophy, and after the push that the attack in Madrid undoubtedly gave, I felt the obligation to do something in this regard, and reader friend, the result is in your hands. I don't want to go without offering my little grain of sand facing the problem that is distressing us. I'll do so, as it could be no other way, from a purely strategic and global focus. The tactics, techniques, the operative formulas, are the privilege of others.

I hope that this special edition is not only a pleasure to read, but that apart from that, you learn a lot from it so that you can protect yourselves and others. Keep it and share it with more people. Don't stop advising others of its existence; when one knows what to do, one immediately becomes a guardian of all. A sole man in the right place makes the difference between a tragedy and life. So, with everyone helping everyone, we will be able to confront more efficiently what is undoubtedly one of the greatest challenges of the new millennium: terrorism.

Hippcrocates! Always Hipprocrates! The winning strategy

I've written it on many occasions and for very distinct motives: the Hippocratic principles are an impeccable way of action in which to confront problems. Master Hippocrates designed a philosophy of action that we can call "the natural way", a philosophy that is founded on three principles that I will not only outline, but will briefly develop: The one who has eyes to see... (and everything else necessary!), well, already knows... those who don't... as much as I might explain it...

1. Do no harm
Not doing harm means not to feed the negative more, cutting its nourishment and growth process. Not doing harm also means that all our actions to confront the conflict, diatribe or problem, do not worsen the overall situation (patient, issue, the planet, etc.) that produces the disease and its symptoms. In Spanish, the word for illness is enfermedad, which comes from the Latin infirmitas. The prefix "in" always indicates negation, and the word "firmitas" means firmness, resistance, strength, obstinacy, perseverance, vigor, power, etc. So, the first measure is to strengthen oneself.

The illness of terrorism can be an opportunity for our societies, acting positively and assertively, to make themselves much stronger; too much given over in the past decades to self-obliging ways, the result has probably caused us to lose strength, perspective, and direction; we can take an already inevitable crisis and see it as an opportunity. We will then act with diligence, immediacy, and with a lot of good sense in this matter.

2. After, clean up

Taking away what is in excess, what tends to develop into a cyst, and saturate oneself with one's own force and dynamic. To clean up what is rotten, contaminated, and contaminating. This at once implies the positive action of adding what is lacking, to re-establish, to balance the whole and with it to modify the phenomenon at its roots, not from its manifestations or symptoms. Remember the principle that everything that tends to cancel out the symptoms will intensify the cause to the same degree, one and the other are really opposites and complimentary.

To balance, it is also necessary to remember that adding the elements of that same force is essential, though being present in excess, are negative. We can put for an example the case of fanaticism; this shouldn't be fought with more fanaticism from the opposing side, rather with another analogous energy, but positive, such as enthusiasm, education (the kind that turns lights on!), creativity, or any other kind of force of that type or degree that the ancient Chinese knew how to situate in that range of forces that they called "fire energy", but in this case, in the positive.

To clean up implies first looking at oneself; it is a conscious act to learn how we have arrived at the situation in question. The one who ignores his past is condemned to repeat it; to get out of the circle of action-reaction implies looking at the things from a superior viewpoint, to see the antagonisms as compliments, to consider unity above the parts, to see what is common in the differences, to polish the unnecessary edges, to adapt flexible and at the same time firm postures.

3. Nature is what cures

When the necessary actions are put into affect and balance is re-established, things, people, and circumstances find their own natural way. Like the Tao, "nothing is done, but nothing remains to be done", the wise man resolves the enigma, transforms reality acting with and in favor of the natural forces, upholding himself by them instead of censoring them.

Paradoxically, peace manifests itself when we establish a permanent state of interior war. When man turns his eyes to the really important things of existence, be it individual or collective, all his or her resources are few when it comes to attending to that which is the true and essential battle front in all of us: life, evolution, the perpetuation of the species are challenges of such magnitude that any other is insignificant by comparison. Creativity, the quest for beauty, harmony, and knowledge are the most noble tasks and challenges to which we can dedicate ourselves, going through this world like the great Indian chief Noah Sealth said, knowing that "the earth doesn't belong to us, rather we belong to it."

"To clean up what is rotten, contaminated, and contaminating. This at once implies the positive action of adding what is lacking, to re-establish, to balance the whole and with it to modify the phenomenon at its roots, not from its manifestations or symptoms"

FROM THE WHOLE AND THE PARTS

"All is one but manifests
itself differentiated."
Lao Tse

The classics give us a marvellous tool of knowledge through what they called the relationship of the elements. The elements are, of course, a representation of reality, a simplification of it that allows us to discern the different states of energy and matter with clarity. Said reduction to the essential has many, many practical applications, but it especially allows us to judge reality from parameters sufficiently objective to compare it to other things and be operative, as well as being sufficiently malleable and flexible to put us in a situation of being able to evaluate any circumstance with the necessary distance.

In the East, said categorizing is done through Yin and Yang, in China, and In and Yo, in Japan, and a whole bunch of different nomenclatures to refer to the same thing, what Nyoity Sakurazawa Osawa called the unifying principle. The complementary opposites are a representation of the cycles of the two essential energies that make up our world, Fire, Yang, and Water, Yin. The cycle of Yin to Yang ascending and the opposite descending, describes the dynamic transformation of the forces. The ancient Chinese decided to describe "seasons" in this context, in what they called the five elements (Go kyo, in Japan), establishing relationships among them.

If we represent the whole as a circle and divide it in two, we will obtain a basic representation of Yin and Yang. Conscious that nothing in nature is straight, this line was represented in a sinuous way; knowing that nothing in it is pure, they included one part of each opposite in the other; aware that everything moves in a spiral, the result was an image that perfectly symbolizes the "perpetuum mobile" of the "Uni-versus", literally, "the One in movement".

In the West, the Greeks bequeathed a division very characteristic of its functional idiosyncrasy, the division into four. They called the aforementioned elements Fire, Earth, Air, and Water, and they represent the warm and cold forces very well, both producing two tendencies in matter, humidity and dryness. The four elements find perfect representation putting a square inside a circle, four defined points in the totality of the "Uni-versus". Compared to the Eastern representation, we must recognize that said image is less dynamic as an image, but there is no doubt that as a symbol, the square inside the circle speaks to us of a tremendously functional compression in which I want to suggest as being the same essence of logic as a tool of consciousness, undoubtedly the most valued treasure that they contributed to humanity.

It's true that logic has totally substituted these ways of describing the world in the past centuries and has imposed its argument as the "only one" acceptable; however, we have been witnessing a recuperation of the others in the past decades, and in my opinion this is the natural result of the exhaustion of reason as the only way. Humans are not only "rational beings"; in fact, we spend our lives making decisions of which the ones reasoned out are the least, and those that are reasonable rarer still. The sentiments, the learned guidelines, the mechanical, and even superstition and the arbitrary often decide far more for us. From this inoperativeness, then, comes the sensation that reason or logic is not sufficient as a way, and if it is so that they are non-substitutable, then so too the traditional formulas that allow us to comprehend and act not only deducing but also inducing conclusions that allow us to act in fields, in many, many fields, in which our scientific preparation is little or non-existent. In order to make this jump in space (a jump which we make every day!) it is, of course, indispensable to consider the learning of this dialectic in a serious way, not like it has come too many times in the past years, and try to move our Cartesian vision of the world toward the use of the knowledge that the traditional wisdom has bequeathed. In books on acupuncture, I frequently discover this defect while I read extensive lists of what Yin is and what Yang is, as if learning the list of the gothic kings were the same as understanding history. This attitude has led many professionals of the needles to wind up limiting themselves to the application of forms and protocols, generally incapable of understanding or explaining that with which they are working, the Yin and Yang energies. This might in part be due to the Westernizing of the knowledge of the traditional East, an inexact translation of the philosophical bases, and of course the absolute establishment of the Western way of seeing the world in our times, as a result of its material success.

It is evident that the quantity of parts into which one wants to divide the Whole represented in the circle, is a decision which depends on the level of the approach to detail that a specific model of a description of the world is able to offer. The division of the One into twelve, for example, would give us the quadrants that astrology studies, when one divides the heavens of the northern hemisphere into twelve "houses" to which correspond the 12 constellations that the sun passes on its apparent movement in the heavens seen from our planet. The cycle begins in the spring equinox when the sun "travels" through the constellation Aries. Each constellation in turn is assigned to one of the four elements, Fire, Earth, Air and Water, which are followed in the horoscope. This division of all into twelve has, of course, become much more popular in the West than the most radical scientists would have liked; such is the power of the traditional formulations, as much as the vision of the world of reason has tried to destroy them. In any case, said divisions can magnificently represent nature and its forces, as well as the way in which they relate to one another, converting themselves, when used well, into extraordinary tools of health, knowledge, and well-being.

Martial Arts are not outside this wisdom, at least those that possess and have known how to preserve the connection with tradition, though it's sure that very few of them, as they are taught in the majority of the cases, are today concerned with the philosophical part. This seems to be an error to me, since said knowledge is not only a differential aspect that very much stands out in our practices, but the majority of potential students are out there hungrily awaiting said knowledge; not in vain, one of the principle reasons why one goes to learn Martial Arts is the quest for one's own identity, what could be described as something just shy of a heroic feat in a globalized world that is full of empty standards.

To limit Martial Arts to a sports event or a self-defense formula, ignoring its cultural and philosophical aspects, is to renounce the potential that they have kept alive and active for centuries, and all of us must make an effort so that such a thing does not happen.

THE SIXTH SENSE

"The truth will make you free,
but before that, it will probably hurt."

The quest for magic as a shortcut to reach extraordinary skills is not exclusive to martial artists; it seems to be a common recourse among human beings. I could be perfectly in agreement with this custom always when we focus ourselves on its root sense, and this isn't its most common interpretation: magic comes from the Latin Magnus, that is, "the great", and for me there is no doubt that the Spanish refrain that says, "He who can do with much can do with little," is a monumental truth. If by magic we focus on that recourse called superstition... of course, I couldn't disagree more. However, it arises that what for some is mumbo jumpo, for others is simply knowledge... there are many things that we don't know, or perhaps it would be more prudent to affirm that there are only a few things we know. From this sensible position and keeping that so very human curiosity active, it is possible that we learn some things in the little period of our existence.

When someone refers to the sixth sense, they try to define a whole group of perceptions that transcend the five known senses. Many of the things we consider extraordinary are not so much so in function of their own nature as of our ignorance in the matter, or of our focus on that catalog that is the perception of the world that we build in our minds from childhood. The perception of the world has allowed us to struggle with our surroundings, imposing ourselves on other creatures, but on the way we have undoubtedly lost other magnificent attributes. There are those who erroneously maintain that such skills aren't so important when they have been lost and substituted by others that are called superior. That is a typical arrogant comment resulting from the perception of the Universe dominated by logic. As an example I'll cite one of these attributes, something simple and basic: the ability to choose those foods that are good for us and reject those that are contaminated or not so good. Nobody who has suffered shell fish poisoning will deny that this would be more than a coveted skill to have had the night before... (especially if you ask them while they are deciding what end of their digestive tube to put in the toilet first!)

It's just that our description of the logical world loves definitions, limits, bounders. Logic is fundamentally in the analysis and this in the division of parts. We say tree and we say: root, trunk, and leaves. But a tree isn't that; a tree is simply a perception. As a painter, I have always been fascinated by the mystery of color and shapes, the beauty of light and shade, the secrets of the three-dimensional, of the depth created on a single plane of two dimensions. Even today I continue being amazed at understanding that what my eyes—and yours, esteemed readers—perceive is only a mental re-creation of the light that objects reflect, and furthermore, exclusively in the vibratory frequencies that our nervous system is capable of perceiving! Everything seems so real but it isn't so. It's like the Matrix parable, we live in and interact with a world that we really don't know the full dimensions of.

I believe that the sixth sense is the excuse, the door by which unusual perceptions are allowed into our minds from the rigid parameters of reason. Reason (of which we are so proud), operates from a central biological computer that works on the basis of routines and sub-routines of learned programs, able to generate new bio-electrical routes, to associate memories, and reach conclusions. Its basic programming is concerned with survival programs that have been created through millions of years of evolution and that establish biological guidelines that have to be obeyed; though reason, that little working of the brain with which we identify so much, doesn't come to understand what is happening.

The sixth sense covers the almost insurmountable distance between reason and biology with lesser or greater success in function of the rigidity with which we stick to a determined description of the world. When we leave the door open, we are better disposed to connect with that other part of our being that possess an innate wisdom.

The body knows things that the mind ignores, it is capable of contributing apparently absurd certainties, of understanding even what is impossible. I have the internal certainty that said mechanisms act in automatic when we disconnect the central controller. The world of dreams is one of those moments wrapped in mystery, but even in wakefulness there are times and events capable of striking the tyrannical state of the central computer and taking control. Critical situations that come out of episodes of temporary amnesia in which the individual does fabulous acts proper of a superman have been perfectly cataloged and witnessed. The drunkard cancels out his frontal lobes and might even stun his reptilian brain, but it is always said that that fall that would kill him in a sober state has practically no effect when he's inebriated. Probably, at the moment of death these automatic systems are also activated and the passage is much nicer than what we have. I can't believe that nature, which has been so generous on other planes, neglects a moment like that, so full of power and mystery.

Martial Arts can develop your sixth sense, you only have to be open to it; if you walk around looking for it... it will slip through your fingers.

"When we leave the door open, we are better disposed to connect with that other part of our being that possess an innate wisdom"

BEING POSITIVE

"A problem is an opportunity dressed in the suit of a mess."

When pressure, tension and problems cease to be in line and pile up; when the energy to confront them declines, the imagination doesn't work and every new thing seems a step further toward a pre-written sentence, then, my friend... it's probably been a while since you have lost the North. How did it all begin? Where did you go wrong?

The chain of negativity always has an uncertain first moment; perhaps that little deviation from the fundamental that with time and space winds up turning into a tremendous going adrift...And it's that the trip, with luck, is long. Paradoxically, the capacity of man to deal with things, perhaps his principle virtue, what has made him prevail, is in a certain sense his greatest curse, to the extent that said persistence can become exactly that which impedes him from learning.

Evolution, that thing that is based on something as simple as an error, only works when it goes beyond the binary "black/white." Everything is more complicated when you come to perceive that in the end everything is an enormous scale of greys in which it is easier to lose oneself. How do you tune your consciousness to maintain the precise judgment? How do you perceive a moving target?

The disciplinary Arts, tradition, gives us the clue: Keep to your center! Close yourself off to dispersion! Open up to experience! Make yourself One with what is apparently beyond you and in so doing unify opposites.

What a difficult task in the times in which we live! However, I don't believe that this would have been essentially easier in an epic or fantasized past, in the end legendary, but neither do I conceive that anyone has the least doubt that acceleration, tension and the extreme forces (radical, if you prefer) of the times in which we live are going to make things any easier. Old tasks in an eternally changing framework.

For that, the old advice about being positive acquires an evermore important dimension. We put into play all the safeguards necessary, that, yes! As long as we don't wind up blind instead of more lucid. This notion of being positive doesn't mean we should be idiots!

Ignoring problems or wanting to ride over them with the idea of simply having good intentions is not a solution. One must be positive while… at the same time one takes the bull by the horns, no matter what the issue is. Every issue has its pointed side, its horn, its sword, its dangerous side, and especially its hidden dagger.

Being positive means to keep a constructive spirit beyond the achievement; as a strategy, as an attitude. Being positive offers us, while facing the inevitable, one more effective and practical disposition. By visualizing, by focusing on the positive aspects of an unfortunate incident, we can also convert a problem into an opportunity ready to be worked at. On the other hand, when darkness traps us, we can never make out an exit; immersed in total darkness, lost in the half-light, focus is impossible… the only thing remaining is to turn the light on. For that, the classics say, "close yourself off to dispersion" and in this way your vitality will increase. Vitality is energy and energy essentially possesses a threshold that inevitably becomes light.

A smile (and what to say about a good belly laugh!) can save your life, focus you on the right distance, offer you a perspective that allows you to confront things, and even transcend the conflict, that is, what allows us to see and integrate its hidden part. The positive offers us the opportunity to look at the same thing with new eyes. Laughing, then, is a great strategy, beginning with oneself! What better way to neutralize instantaneously our personal importance? And it's only by feeling ourselves important that we can get depressed, only by giving ourselves importance can we suffer.

When we put problems in appropriate agreement, the difficulties are nothing more than an irritating horn blown by a little devil in the middle of an enormous symphony orchestra. Why do we want to listen to nothing else but that instrument? Being positive implies listening to the whole symphony, including that irritating horn, that much is true! Perhaps until we discover that its sound doesn't lack meaning in the harmony as whole! Then we move on… and soon we wind up liking it!

Being positive is a great strategy, always when you don't permit yourself to fall into the Naïve. And what is more naïve that to judge things form the point of view of "good and bad?" When what one tries to do is oppose the positive with the negative, negating the dark side of things, one irredeemably enters into a contradictory dialogue;

one is not unify the opposites, one is confronting them! This is the figure of the sanctimonious, of the fundamentalist who tries to transcend without having integrated, and of course, making of the "good," sooner or later, an inevitable "bad." No. This is not the way of the man of knowledge, of the Warrior, the way from which whispers the advice of the wise men who have existed in the world.

The paradox of our reality, the game of opposites that are complementary, makes of our plane of Consciousness and Being a game of subtle chiaroscuro, tones, colors, and forms enormously rich and complex. And it is in that richness where its charm lies; it is in its danger, in its uncertainty, where the wise man savors that rich and incomparable nectar of fluidity, of the realization of the consciousness of the mystery of the One and the thousand parts. In order to understand this mystery on a day to day basis, one has to operate from the first principle that tradition advises us: Keep to your center. It is a gigantic paradox, but only from the center will we be able to discern the periphery with clarity. One of the mysteries of the Universe is that we, our very creation, has allowed us in the end to look at ourselves; admiring one's beauty, one's splendor, one's greatness and power. Does there exist any experience more "religious," more transcendent that this?

The positive is a direction chosen on our road toward the infinite. How do you discover if you are using it adequately? There's nothing easier! Always when the choice of positive leads you to determine that you are walking forward, upward, within and toward the All... do not doubt. Your compass is working!

> **"One of the mysteries of the Universe is that we, our very creation, has allowed us in the end to look at ourselves; admiring one's beauty, one's splendor, one's greatness and power.**
> **Does there exist any experience more 'religious,' more transcendent that this?"**

BUSINESS AND MARTIAL ARTS?

(Referring to Martial Arts...)
"This is my hobby,
but of course I'm not against the benefits."
(A new friend)

Marketing, business, bartering are all an essential part of the social habits of human nature. One only has to observe the success that its implantation has had all over the planet in order to understand that it must be based on something very solid, on something fundamentally inscribed in our most elemental codes. To do business is, after all, a response to the natural law of balance, the same as in that in physics known as the law of the connected test tubes. But, before all else, this interchange is an essentially mercurial activity. Mercury, the god with winged feet, the god of communication and the verb, moved around (like the planet that received his name) at great speed, carrying messages from one side to the other. And when one travels, one quickly discovers that that which is plentiful in one place is usually not highly valued, while it will necessarily be very appreciated wherever it is scarce... it is only necessary to exchange it, to be capable of taking it from one place to another. The added value of such management is the base of business.

They were called "mercurials" in the esoteric and cryptic language of the alchemists, those elements capable of acting as principles of transportation of information of other more active or reactive elements from nature, but unable to move by themselves. Said function allowed for exchange and the enrichment of the material and its functions, grouping themselves in more and more complex units. Without the mercurial, life as we understand it would be impossible.

The old fathers of our culture, the Greeks and Romans, quickly understood the essence of these forces, awarding them a place of privilege in their Olympus. The Greek goddess Athena, the Roman goddess Minerva, the wise and temperate warrior born from the head of Zeus himself was, in fact, the custodian of the traders just as she was protector of knowledge, business, industry and trade. Her figure was probably born infected to a great extent by the Phoenician ways and by their gods since men always create in line with themselves. The air, the same that filled the sails of the travelers, has always been the element that best represented the nature of Mercury;

thoughts, always faster than actions, also fell under his regency; of course, letters, writing, communication, poetry, exist under the dominium (de domus = house) of the same gods and participate in their same changing, modulating, unpredictable and curious essence.

However, this same inclination is not appreciated in all cultures. Those that are more closed to difference have always shared two antagonistic mercurial tendencies. Isolation and lack of communication always coincide with the low intensity of trading activities. The rejection of them has too often created a sub-culture that rejects everything that represents or symbolizes this principle.

I have observed that this matter is not always understood in the martial environment. Some of its most traditionalist elements support each other in a feeling probably inherited from the Samurai caste (not essentially different from what happened with the feudal lords of Medieval Europe and their rejection of the "vile metal"), a custom that in both cases accelerated their decline and their era. The arrogance that upheld those positions was able to survive encrusted in many of their rituals and some of their most sublime principles, like aloofness, have nonetheless been misunderstood and distorted.

It is understandable that the negative aspects of trade, usury, taking advantage beyond the limits of replacement (exhausting resources), profiting (but at the loss of another), or any form of abuse, opportunism, or deceptive speculation, are scornful attitudes, but one can't judge an activity, principle, or element only for its dark or negative aspects. Even the element of fire is saved from this burning! Fire can destroy, consume, devastate, but it can also heat, transform, sublimate and clean so that life is renewed.

What is certain is that many people from the martial environment relate badly to the business end of their activities and they live in a perpetual state of contradiction between their desire to fill up their classes and that of living thoughtfully and thriving in their favorite activity. Such friction is frequently manifested in outbursts of "purism" on those occasions in which I have had to speak with them about advertising, marketing plans, etc., for their school, association, federation, or dojo. It is hard for them to understand the positive side of the mercurial energy and they prefer to hand themselves over to the hands of Mars before succumbing to the temperate charm of Athena. As far as I understand it, this is one of the principle reasons for the extinction of a lot of old and wise thoughts, schools, and Arts that have succumbed to their own entropy and death, exhausted in their own lack of communication, self-censorship, "purism" and secrecy.

But, dear readers, let me confess. Mine is not an impartial judgment. As a Gemini, I am (constellation governed by Mercury) in a genuinely mercurial profession (writer, editor, businessman, and communicator), I believe in the goodness of communication, of thought, and of exchange, whether of goods or of knowledge. Since I created this magazine, I have confronted this on multiple occasions (and many times frontally), where I have perceived obscurantism, concealment, or the projected arrogance of exclusivity. From the first day, we have insisted on opening the doors and windows of this little world: we wonder about this or that, we get in touch with these and those, we diffuse extracting unknown Arts from the catacombs, we question those who know and we open ourselves up to novelty, however strange or unsettling it might seem to us, since it is the good judgment of each one that must decide what is positive and what one wants to incorporate into one's life.

There is no contradiction whatsoever between living doing what you like, prospering, making money and following your path as a true Warrior. Once again, the answer is not so much in having (or not having) as it is in just being. The ascetic image of the warrior monk is an archetype that can take root and so subjugate the spirit, encouraging personal importance and arrogance, its opposite image. It is stupid to presume that one's own image is a pure, aloof way when reality shows us these people mooring themselves to that same way with desperation, terrified by the idea that placing a foot outside their safe and protected uterine space might lead to making a mistake. Errare humanum est! my friends.. .And this is the essence of what is human... I'm sorry. Apart from there being nobody to blame, a warrior always takes the responsibility for his own acts.

Business, not as negation of entertainment, but as an creative exchange based on an appropriate sense of the just; of opportunity (synchrony) as opposed to opportunism; of production as opposed to speculation; of ingenious exchange that enriches both parts, without deceit, nor abuses, these are very noble ways to go through this world, taking what is necessary to realize your dreams as a person, but also as a martial artist. Knowing how to reconcile these two worlds—which are really one—only requires seeing things with perspective.

Everything in nature requires the mercurial in order to exist. Don't hold back, there is only to do it with impeccability.

GICHIN FUNAKOSHI
We analyze the twenty golden rules of the founder of Karate-Do

Gichin Funakoshi was not only the founder of Karate-Do, the one who systemized it, but he also knew how to imbue this Art with his own sense of life. The techniques and rudiments of Karate-Do already existed, as is known, when Funakoshi organized it into a coherent whole; it was the vision and the personal commitment of his character that managed to give strength and a global meaning to a style that has consecrated itself as one of the Martial Arts references across the planet. For this reason, getting to know the conceptualization of Funakoshi's Karate is not an effort in vain. Surely, these days Karate students know little about the original formulas of their Art; perhaps the notion of this article to resuscitate the primordial dictates of the Master even strike some as anachronistic, but those who don't know their past can only poorly confront the future.

Funakoshi was a man with a very special personality. To get to know Funakoshi as an individual, his personality, there's nothing better than to read his autobiography: "Karate-Do My Way", fortunately translated into almost every language. In it we find a simple man, not an intellectual. A man with a straight and defined moral doctrine with some principles that define a strong dorsal fin from which arises a strong character loyal to his convictions. Undoubtedly, it couldn't have been easy to deal with him in life; however, he was one of those magnetic personalities, a born leader, who knew how to transmit his message to those around him by making a strong impression. And though the Art that he defined in its forms and principles is not much like what today we know as Karate, it is no less sure that its evolution would have been impossible without a strong and firm starting point such as that which the master was able to imprint on the way of the empty hand.

For this, it is essential to understand one of the main legacies compiled in his Dojo Kun; twenty principles that define the formal formulation and attitude that must preside over the practice of the Art in order for the student to reach excellence. In the old days, these principles were recited out loud before each class, a lost practice even in the most traditional dojos. Recited like a litany, the students knew them by heart and even without understanding them; in their practice, their meanings and reasons for existing were integrated little by little.

The article that we publish today tries to go into the meaning and hidden reasons behind these twenty points in order to facilitate to the youngest ones a deeper, more complete understanding of the essential origins of their Martial Art and to remember the best, as much in age as in experience, the origin, the fundamentals of our Martial tradition.

Funakoshi, a man of few words and of less explanations, maintained that that which you learn with your body you never forget, while that which you learn with your head is easy to forget. This is absolutely true, but undoubtedly the Master couldn't have imagined that in the years to come the head would wind up serving in too many cases for little more than to put a hat on. For this, without refuting the founder, we understand that it is essential to delve into the essences of Karate, analyzing one by one the points and their meanings, an inheritance full of value, now and always, one more gift from the founder to whom we Karatecas always owe respect and gratitude.

1. Karate-Do begins and ends with the greeting

Gentleness and respect are also demonstrated and acquired with their practice. To greet is to remind our body that it must obey some criteria in which respect must subjugate other impulses that are undoubtedly activated in the practice (aggression, fear, etc.). To restrain them is one of the tasks of the Martial Art.

But beyond the courtesy, the Eastern greeting of dropping the head has a symbolic meaning and even an energetic one that is not very widespread, or what is the same, very much forgotten. At nodding the head, as much in Seiza position as when standing, we unify the principles of Heaven and Earth, the principles and their energies that penetrate our body through the spine (crown of the head and genitals) like two strong serpents. When in Seiza, the hands must be united at the same time (not one first and the other after) leaving a triangle formed between the thumbs and index of the hands between those that must be placed in front.

Courtesy means restraint in order to re-direct instinct; its repetition is always educative and helps organize the hierarchies. The greeting to the master has this sense. The salute with your adversary re-forms the formal space of the combat providing this with limits, reminding us that the enemy is within, not outside. The other is only a mirror, an opportunity to realize this, something in which our limitations will be seen to be reflected; he is not the one guilty of them.

2. You will not use Karate-Do without motive

Sun Tzu begins his book on war advising us, "War is a matter of vital importance, the territory of life and death mustn't be confronted lightly." Validating aggression is a philosophically complex matter. For Funakoshi, aggression is only explained as an act of defense. Unwarranted violence was continuously criticized by the Master, even opposed to the practice of Ju Kumite (free fighting), which his son defended. Even further, Karate is training of the personality, of the spirit of the student, who trains his character and his body to reach a state of alertness and excellence, not to boast about his skills or to demonstrate anything to himself or others.

3. Practice Karate-do with a sense of justice

Reinforcing the previous point, the Master further adds that the practice of Karate and its use must only serve for just causes, with impeccable attitudes. At the same time, on this point Funakoshi advises us about those who try to use Karate and its knowledge to serve ignoble causes. For the teachers, the selection of students and their intentions in learning the Art were one of the principle concerns and if today the powerful gentleman who is Mr. Money has lowered the standards in a way that only limits entrance to those who pay, it is good to remember that we have an acquired responsibility in the exercise of teaching the Art.

4. Before knowing others, we must know ourselves

Just as the text that is inscribed on the portal at the Oracle of Delphi pronounces, "Know thyself", Funakoshi establishes here one of the essential principles of the Way of the Warrior. "Nothing does anything to anyone!" Instead of hiding behind the continuous blaming of others for the negative circumstances in our lives, Funakoshi impels us to look inward, firstly, and in this way assume responsibility for our acts. Instead of losing time trying to escape our miseries by pointing to those separate from us, the master demands rigor in our judgements. First look at yourself, after, at yourself and after that at yourself again, and after having looked once more at yourself, consider others.

5. From the technique intuition is born

This is a principle that is frequently misinterpreted in the West. Many understood that it is the technique in and of itself that is important; however, we must begin with the knowledge that for the Oriental, the value of things is in its form. The cup exists and has usefulness to the extent that it possesses an empty space. The wheel turns and keeps its structure because it has space between the spokes.

The technique is then "the form" that directs us to the natural movement, not a tightened girdle that strangles our fluidity; however, to reach said ability, it is necessary to train the technique so that in the end our knowledge is bonded with "the natural". In this way, Funakoshi reminds us that the practice of a correct technical form will connect us with our essential knowledge, with our intuition, help us flow naturally with the infinite circumstances.

6. Don't let the spirit meander

Concentration is, in all Oriental practice, an inescapable principle. When the hard training puts enough pressure on the mind, it tends to meander, to detach itself in order to interrupt the effort. Funakoshi was a man of customs and of solid and ordered principles, one who knew that everything begins in Yin. To stay in the here and now is essential for the practice of Karate as a way of consciousness.

The routine and the repetitions of training are a tough test for concentration. The student must avoid mental dispersion and the mechanization of the movement. Only being present within it will the techniques possess the adequate force and intensity; only by being concentrated on its application can we recharge our systems of force to finish the training session stronger than when we started.

7. Failure is born from negligence

For the Master, there are no coincidences, there are no "Buts...", nor "It's just that..." With this point the Master reinforces the previous one, attention and commitment are essential in the practice. To not adequately attend to the parts that make up the whole, to do it deficiently, without due attention, or without the necessary effort, leads to failure. Failure is not a disgrace that arbitrarily falls from the sky, rather it is always the result of a lack of attention, not being careful, abandonment, laxity, apathy, or slovenliness. Funakoshi reminds us that we are responsible for our acts and of their results, in this way opening the door to the possibility of improvement and growth. Evolution exists through precise and continuous error, for that the warrior gets up every time he falls with the certainty that if he corrects his error he will be able to reach his objective.

8. Karate-do is only practiced in the Dojo

The "Do Jo" is literally "the place of awakening". Karate do is not a practice to hit in the street, its objective is not to make others submit rather to reshape oneself, to wake up to a reality where the symbolic and the real become one thing. Furthermore, with this principle the Master reminds all of us once more that we mustn't use our knowledge inadequately, limiting our practice to the sacred space of the Do Jo.

9. The practice of Karate-do is for life

As a spiritual practice, Karate-do is an Art that forms a part of the nature of the students forever. Apart from reciting this phrase, the students renewed their commitment to the Art daily, giving it the adequate space in their beings. As a practice of long and slow results, Karate requires a lasting commitment in order to reach its objectives and open the veil that hides its treasures, and this is why the Master repeats this principle of a commitment for life.

10. Deal with problems in the spirit of Karate-do

Once again, we understand through another principle that Karate Do as an Art transcends the sphere of the merely physical or sportive. Karate is a way of living, a way to confront things. When Funakoshi tells us to deal with problems with the spirit of Karate Do, he reminds us that we are warriors twenty-four hours a day, not only the time we are on the tatami. In this way, Karate Do is interwoven with all the everyday events in the existence of the neophyte in such a way that the virtues that adorn it must be activated in the face of adversity with self-control, responsibility, will power, respect and commitment.

11. Karate-do is like boiling water

Water is a re-occurring and essential motif in the Japanese tradition. There are two hundred different terms to say water depending on the state and circumstances that surround it. Water is the beginning of life and the essence of its nature, it goes downward, flows, surrounds, doesn't oppose.

When Funakoshi cites water en its boiling state, he is speaking about its wooden state in so far as this makes reference to the five elements, called Go Kyo in Japan. Wood is characterized by being the force of will and boiling water converts itself into the opposite realization of its nature. Activated in this way, it rises instead of going down in the process of evaporation. This activation of the nature of water is the fire of consciousness that arises from the effort of the neophyte. For that, the practitioner must be capable of remaining in a fluid but active state, always ready to respond to an attack.

12. Don't nourish the idea of defeating nor that of being defeated

It is this point that has so controversially generated the debate over whether Karate should or should not be practiced in competition. In my opinion, the essential matter in this arises in the correct attitude of the student. If we put the objective outside, undoubtedly we don't have it inside. But such a decision is more a state of mind than a defined act. For the Master, Karate is before all else an interior way. As a road of overcoming oneself, in Karate, the external achievements cannot be its foundation; therefore, the enemy is not outside but inside; as long as we attend to the external we won't be attending to the real reason that the Art exists, and for that he reminds us: Be careful! Not that way! So, don't throw more wood on the fire!

13. Adapt the attitude of the opponent

One must avoid pre-conceived formulas in life. Be flexible, adapt oneself to the forever changing circumstance; the Master reminds us that we must adapt to them. The practice of the Art is not an application of formulations but the securing of the necessary resources in order to constantly flow beyond our limitations. "Every bull has its fight!" states the bullfighting saying, and for that, those who try to always use the same technique facing distinct opponents will be defeated.

14. The secret of combat resides in the art of knowing how to direct it

Combat, as Sun Tzu says, is a whole where apparent disorder reins; however, the expert understands the hidden secrets that are ordering it. Directing is possible in the middle of apparent chaos always when we understand not only that an order exists, but that it can be directed from the center. Understanding that it is the center of the spiral which directs its periphery, as much in space as in time, is the Master Key that Funakoshi proposes, reminding us that such a thing is possible, telling us to look for those essential rhythms that dominate all conflicts in order to make ourselves the owners of the rhythm of the opponent so that he dances to our rhythm.

15. The hands and feet must strike like sables

Here, the Master reinforces the knowledge of spirals as the most powerful and natural forces and movements. Einstein opened our eyes at comprehending and affirming that the shortest distance between two points would never be straight. The very formation of our arms comes in the embryonic period of two spirals that come from the collision of the Heaven and Earth forces that generate the embryo. In its polarization, which is growth, these forces develop two pairs of spirals of seven turns that generate the arms and the legs. One is longer, Yin, (the legs) and the other is shorter, Yang (the arms); its conception and architecture make all circular movement easier. The Japanese sable is curved for this reason, compared to the majority of Western swords. The understanding of the principles in the spiral is deeply inscribed in the popular knowledge in the East and frequently represented in its symbols. The master reminds us with this principle that we must act in accord with the nature of things and not against them, opening with this key the door to a principle to which every student must pay attention in his own learning, a secret to remember beyond what his Master teaches him.

16. At crossing the threshold of our home, 10,000 enemies are waiting

Again, we have the principle of continuous attention. Attention must close itself off to entropy and there's nothing better for that than to put oneself to the test, and for that the Master teachers us his trick. Always be on guard! In this way your attention will remain alert. The Vietnamese used to repeat to themselves, "The one who awaits the worst never loses the initiative." But, please, without paranoia!

I don't know why, but this rule always brings to mind an Eastern saying that I love: "If a tiger guards the ravine, ten thousands deer will not pass!"

17. Kamae is the rule for the beginner, later it is possible to adopt a more natural posture

Kamae! To be on guard, attentive, willing, ready to react. With this affirmation, the Master reminds us that the training has grades and evolution. The training is like a funnel through which you pass, stretching your nature and ridding yourself of the unnecessary in order to return to yourself, but transformed by the experience. It is a way to return to what is natural, a round trip in which your luggage can't be carried, your memories, your experiences. I remember on this point a Zen saying: "Before Zen, the mountain is mountain, the valley, valley, the moon, moon. During Zen, the mountain is no longer a mountain, nor the valley a valley, nor the moon a moon. After Zen, the mountain returns to being a mountain, the valley, a valley, and the moon... moon." Nothing has changed and yet everything is different!

Once trained, Kamae is an attitude, a key that opens a door, not the room in which you are trying to enter; it is the finger that points to the moon, not the moon itself!

18. The kata must be done correctly; however, in real combat their movements will be adapted to the circumstances

As before, he tells us to be flexible but rigorous. The Kata are the base of the "form", for that it is essential that in their practice one trains the movements with technical perfection. There is no contradiction between this and to fight with movements that do not reproduce what one executes in the Kata, as some current masters proclaim. Funakoshi left this point very clear. Once more, we must remember the position that Orientals maintain with respect to the forms and that we developed in the analysis of the first point of the Dojo Kun. The intention of Karate Do is not that of creating extreme fighters, or supermen, rather to develop the spirit and the body of the student through training that gets the best out them, facilitating the positive education and growth of the individual, who can, in addition, make positive contributions to their respective societies.

19. Three factors must be considered: Strength, magnitude, and technical level

Facing a partner or facing an opponent, Funakoshi reminds us of three factors that we must keep in mind in evaluating what we have in front of us and ourselves. The first two relate to physical considerations and the third to experience and knowledge.

20. Go deeply into your thinking

Probably back then, as now, Karate students were people more of action than of reflection. But as everything must be seen in its opposite, the Master finishes his proposals with a clear allusion to the mental development of the neophytes. On this plane of reality, all is mind, or in the words of Carlos Castaneda, the world is a description. It is not in vain, then, to tell all practitioners of Karate Do to develop their skills and knowledge so that they can grow as people, understanding the reality that underlies appearances, reflecting and meditating to complete their learning.

Funakoshi still lives in his proposal

In this analysis we have seen that the Karate Do that its founder proposes is a transcendent practice to the extent that it can take us beyond the symbolic, a way that opens doors and windows to allow us to understand and act justly, even beyond moral evaluations. A way of interior growth that stems from the exterior with positive results, a formulation of the way of the warrior that has known how, in one way or another, to find an echo almost unthinkable in those early days in which the Master combined the thousand-year-old warrior tradition with the understanding and the initiation formulas from the Japanese tradition in order to reach a formula as universal as it is intense, one that has survived, evolved and transformed thousands of people in the past decades.

Although today his principles shown in the Dojo Jun remain ignored, they are alive in the spirit that underlies the diverse practices of the multiple styles, transformations and polarizations of the same initial spiral; a firm starting point that had a name: Gichin Funakoshi. So, Oh, Master, with this article we want to renew for you our eternal gratitude and recognition, and nothing better to do it that to think about you when so many students think that you are antiquated. What they do not know yet is that what is classic is eternal and can never be antiquated.

**"Funakoshi,
a man of few words and of
less explanations,
maintained that that which
you learn with your body you
never forget, while that which
you learn with your head is
easy to forget"**

MARTIAL CULTURES

It is surprising when one has to deal with so many countries how it comes to be understood that there is no single "Martial Culture" in these times, but many co-existent and distinct ones, curiously in the most absolute ignorance of each other.

There is great variety of organizational models in all that concerns the world of Martial Arts, but we can establish two absolutely contrasting ones, the French model and the North American. The first is the heir to the Napoleonic vision of a great interventionist state in civil society; the second, a space of freedoms in which the order of the day is, "Anything goes."

It is evident that, like all opposites, these models are complementary, but to continue generalizing (today I can't even deal with myself!), the virtue, perhaps, is found in the middle, far from the two extremes.

I feel a great admiration for Napoleon, that great general, that little man in whose head fit an entire empire. More Latin than Corsican than his chauvinistic admirers would like, Napoleon took the French Revolution to the paroxysm of its own contradictions, establishing at that critical juncture the basis of the modern state. Its "secondary effects" are still alive in the legislation of the French Republic, and even in the design of the streets of Paris (sufficiently wide so that the artillery can defend them; we mustn't forget that he was an artilleryman!).

The MA in France are controlled and organized by the National Federations and whoever is not in one of them simply doesn't exist. To give classes in France requires the approval of the State, it doesn't matter if in your country you are "the top" in, let's say, "Japanese archery", or "Gypsy knife"... you had better negotiate with whoever is responsible for the creation of a department in a recognized Federation or you don't have a chance.

On the more positive side of the issue, the government with its budgets and support of the martial activities as sportive concerns, undoubtedly involves enormous facility in achieving fantastic results in competition, with the creation of high-level, international sports teams, as well as social recognition of said activities as a common good at a level that is not found in any other place. In the shadow of these Federations, little minority factions flourish as they can with a greater or lesser non-sportive or cultural meaning, which try to develop their activities under an umbrella that is barely has form. Creativity is continually put to the test for many styles that determinedly seek a place in the country; in exchange, the citizen knows with certainty that everything that is announced must answer to some canon behind which the State always appears as guarantor, with police putting restrictions on it.

Then we have the American model, curiously direct heir in its fundamentals and in its constitution to the French revolution through an uncountable number of national heroes, almost all of them masons, much more lovers of Montesquieu than Robespierre (you only have to look at the symbols and inscriptions that still exist today on the dollar bill!). This is a model of modern democracy in which the State must only be a guarantor of the freedom of its citizens, and intervene the least possible in its initiatives. Without a doubt, this attitude was strongly established to the extent that the "pioneering fathers" arrived to the country fleeing the abuse of the institutions, as much religious as governmental, of old Europe, and they were not willing to do "more of the same" there where, with so many hardships, they were settling. Such determination acquired body and judicial structure with such diligence that even today it leads to formulas of behavior that continue to surprise the inhabitants on the other side of the Atlantic; formulas that many times are censored, with the mistaken argument of the antiquity of its cultures. This, it seems, concedes on them a privilege of some kind as to what is good and what isn't. But antiquity, by itself, is not a guarantee of anything; if it were so, we should go back to establishing the "droit du seigneur", or some other not very edifying tradition when seeing the morals in the XXI century.

But let's return to the North American model of organization, a model that can be summed up in one phrase: "Organize yourselves." Here there is no money for Federations, so that the Federations must look for their own money. This puts a lot of pressure on adventurers and some undoubtedly get lost in the known attitude of "for money, anything goes." It is no less certain that the money allocated by the governments in function of the quantity of people signed up for a federation or the results in competition is the creator of power struggles and foolishness without end in the Federations called "official".

In America, any organization can act as long as it doesn't go against any other law of the State, and of course, if it pays its taxes. Undoubtedly, this formula stimulates freedom of action and private initiative, but on the other hand, the citizen must learn to defend himself alone against charlatans and swindlers of all kinds, who make their fortunes based on the laws of the market. Without the existence of common measures and references for things, both extremes are produced: magnificent individuals like Bruce Lee can exist and develop their work with freedom. And the opposite: individuals of very dubious capacity and knowledge selling their certificates of who knows how many black belts of styles as much unheard of as extravagant (have you ever heard of Eskimo Karate?) by postage-free mail without any control whatsoever.

There is always the other side of the coin. And it is evident that both things co-exist and are developed in this environment so little understood in old Europe, so criticized... and at the same time, so admired. Can you imagine Bruce Lee trying to create a department in a French Federation to be able to give official classes in the country?

Everything has its reasons for existing in this world, the problem is that to ignore one's own origins (to say nothing of those of others!) in order to perpetuate emotional visions based on nationalism continues being one of the obscurantisms that in our day we've probably been dragging along since the nineteenth century. There is no perfect model and to try to defend one or the other to death, as I've seen in some conversations between specialists, is a demonstration of historic blindness as well as outdated chauvinism. We are all heirs to a past that conditions us. It is our job in the present to try to correct the errors and vices that each formula has undoubtedly held since its beginning.

Probably neither of the two models is the perfect one and it would be necessary to dive into an intermediate formula with common sense, which would preserve the possibility for a new Bruce Lee to give birth to his creature in a stimulating, free, and generous breeding ground while assuring that anyone without documents finds sufficient difficulties in his attempts to fool the unsuspecting (who, on the other hand, deserves it for being a loony or an idiot!), those capable of believing that about "learn Karate by mail in ten lessons"... Believe me: There is no room for even one more idiot in this world!

America would do well to learn from the magnificent sports results that the great styles obtain in countries with much smaller population but where sports have reached an exceptional level of participation and sophistication. The high-performance Italian Karate Federation installations, to give an example, the technical level of their trainers and experts, amaze those citizens from the Americas who go there. What to say about Taekwondo in Spain, that can give even the Koreans a hiding, or French Judo, a sport of the masses in the country, etc., etc.... these and many other achievements can't be ignored.

On the other hand, phenomena like Bruce Lee or the Gracie revolution never would have been able to develop and mature in Europe; Vale Tudo, MMA, free fight... if they'd depended on Europe, they wouldn't have seen the light yet. America is undoubtedly a creative space, the breeding ground where everything interacts, measures itself, is maximized. Europe is too restricted and predisposed to prohibit what isn't on the menu. This insistence is tremendously castrating and oppressive in such a way that the one who dares to move him or herself, not only doesn't show up in the photo, but if they catch him, they cut him out.

Budo International is a transnational medium, standard bearer of a new vision, of a new unifying paradigm between both sides of the Atlantic that tries to lead to a meeting among the lovers of the sector, of course impossible in any other magazine. Those who criticize us in staunch and limited speeches, those who take pleasure admiring themselves in the contemplation of their own naval, as much on one side as the other, perhaps believe that the universe is a circle; but no friends! For the modern warriors, for those who know how to look at this phenomenon with vision, for this magazine, this universe seems much more like a sphere.

SILENCE

"When decrease acts persistently, it surely acts on increase."
From the I Ching (The Book of Changes)

We live immersed in continuous background noise, a sound that turns toward tones more or less acute that are more and more intense and omnipresent each day, so much so that frequently it winds up taking the role of the soloist in the orchestra of our own songs, to the point of making us forget that which is our own tune.

In the symphony of life, we all enjoy our own and unique tune. It is a song that is familiar (stricto sensu), tuned to the vibratory key of humans, of the Planet, of our times, and this time that is ours, fellow humans, is that of acceleration. The accelerated vibrations turn like light at its maximum, and ours is a vibratory universe. What we perceive of it is no more than a representation that offers us the capacities of our senses, which despite being very useful for specific questions, have been influenced by the way in which the central computer has decided to process them.

In the tragedy provoked by the tsunami that devastated the coasts of Southeast Asia, the scientists verified with surprise that despite finding themselves in the place of the catastrophe, a great number of domesticated livestock, as well as wild animals in abundantly populated natural and protected areas, survived, with virtually no loss of life among them, which was undoubtedly a great relief and something that avoided an even worse health situation through the contamination of the water.

What made those animals leave the area in question and go someplace safe? No, this is not the only case in which we have verified the connection that animals have with the environment; a relationship that is not, as is the case with us, questioned by an educated mind. It is rather a symbiosis, a kind of uniqueness, a continuous and inseparable interrelation, something that undoubtedly we had and that we have relegated to second place by way of the service we pay to other skills. Such uniqueness (to which we have called instinct, accustomed as we are to putting names to everything in our personal catalog), is not a skill, strictly speaking; it is not an "addition"; rather it is a "remains" from the background noise that our own catalog of the world generates. It is the mental silence of the animals that allows them to listen to the "Planet's song", and the most difficult from among all, according to the Lakota, is the "song of the stone".

To silence our minds is an act of immense power for a human; trying it in a continuous way allows us to take a giant step in our consciousness of Being and unexpectedly offers us a new point of reference to judge ourselves and confront the world with temperance and perspective. All the initiating ways go through that station on their trajectory toward true knowledge. To stop the world, to detain the unstoppable river of our thoughts, might seem simple; it would be enough "to not do", but everything in our education has led us to continual learning through squandered action, followed by the verification of the effects of it, the correction, if it comes, and once the method is found, its perpetuation in the search for efficient routines, which, if we insist, we manage to purify until achieving said efficiency.

In Martial Arts we have learned from the first day of class that our body follows parameters in its learning, routines and sub-routines based on the initial overflow, as if we were imitating the Big Bang. How easy it would be if we could make our students understand that when one tries to put force into a strike, one must be capable of completely inhibiting the antagonistic muscles, and that the power comes from the coordinated combination of the whole body united in support of said action, capable of tensing in only one moment in order to create power in the final projection of the movement. But we all insist on tensing all the muscle groups in the object zone of the movement, letting some hinder others until we exhaust ourselves. The continuous repetitions, so frequent in the teaching of almost all the styles, allow us to comprehend by forcing us to continue the action (with no choice!) that the muscles are more capable of efficiently executing the orders if we neutralize part of them and re-direct the energy to others. Then the nerve synapses find new paths to execute our commands with more efficiency and with less waste. When seen in this way, it doesn't seem to be a very intelligent learning system, don't you agree? However, it is tremendously effective when used well.

Perhaps some of you have had the chance to experience what is called "beginner's luck." A guy who has never been in an Irish pub has a few pints and invited to participate in a game of darts, goes and gets a bull's eye at the first try. Ahh! Luck? I don't believe in luck. I think that our body knows more than we could accept, or said in another way, more than our minds can perceive, and once this is silenced, for an instant we are capable of doing heroic deeds that we are, of course, incapable of repeating, though clearly to the extent the mind insists on it.

Mental silence implies an absence of intention; the difficult simplicity of the natural occurs only in this way, for which, and this is a mysterious paradox, it can't be looked for intentionally; and for that the neophytes must concentrate on the execution of the technique. This is most of all a pretext of the true Master in order to offer the spirit of the student the opportunity to discover the emptiness from which all things come, not mechanizing their movements, rather executing them by being totally present in the here and now, tightening the rope of the mind in such a way that in a given moment the miracle can occur that we totally empty ourselves of intention, and in the worlds of Master Awa, "It shoots."

In the end, if you observe, this process very much resembles the system we physically utilize for learning: tons of effort… in order to discover that the secret is a lot closer to, not so much not making an effort as when we stop trying to make an effort, in order to reach the naturalness of abandoning all intention at last.

Of course, these concepts are complex and require an indispensable sophistication of the intention and sensitivity of the practitioner. They are not for everyone, though anyone could access them if they tried, not letting themselves be seduced by the sirens of the tangible… but what is certain is that our commands and the very acceleration of the times in which we live give incentive for the use of and search for paradigms of mechanical efficiency, mechanized and mechanizing (homo est maquina): effectiveness of immediate consumption, effectiveness in record time, goals that are too difficult and defined for one to be able to take the necessary time to do something so "useless" as stop the tireless flow of our accelerated thoughts and their unmistakable humming…

If we reduce the Martial practices to mere technical executions and do not take care of those other more subtle aspects, we will no doubt be losing the "lion's share" of the matter, just as we are negating the possibility of making them ways to realize that eternal part, so present and so evasive at the same time, which continuously and silently call us in the middle of our noisy existence, offering us a haven of peace, always at hand in the middle of the worst mess.

To be conscious of the Mystery, with capital letters, that hides and lies in wait at every instant of our lives can be a good first step on our road toward knowledge; toward the understanding that only from silence can we adjust our own and unique song, tuning in with the melodies of the Earth and Heaven and revealing through them the great secret.

"To silence our minds is an act of immense power for a human; trying it in a continuous way allows us to take a giant step in our consciousness of Being and unexpectedly offers us a new point of reference to judge ourselves and confront the world with temperance and perspective"

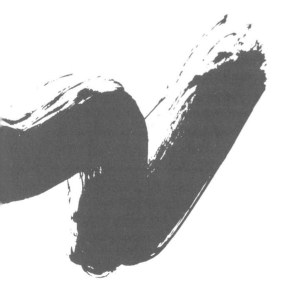

SEX AND VIOLENCE

While I write these lines I visualize you, reader friends. I see you rushing into these paragraphs, touched by the most natural of curiosities. Even those who always skip over the editorial page, these two magic words will have caught your attention, perhaps for the first time—and I hope not the last—and you will venture to accompany me to the end in this space for reflection that I am very happy to share with you every month.

Sex and violence are truly two powerful forces that often go hand in hand. Every culture could be defined by the ways in which they deal with these two matters, or in another way, by the way in which the culture represses, re-directs, organizes, or sublimates both questions in their behavioral codes.

No one will be amazed at this stage if I begin this essay referring to the Greco-Latin classics and to their definitions of both principles in mythology. Without a doubt, Mars represents violence and Venus sex. Even today, their symbols are utilized to represent man and woman (Guess which is which!) and there are not a few books out there that deal with the theme using these analogies; such is its appropriateness.

Mars, as I've written on previous occasions, is a god that is born without the intervention of a masculine principle, which is a curious paradox if we keep in mind that that is precisely what he represents. The Mars principle is impetuous, not reflexive, throwing energy into action, violent, preeminent, proud. His labor, according to the astrologers, is in defending the Sun, the essential 'I', from external attacks that life itself involves. Violence, as an opportune defense, is perfectly acceptable in the majority of cultures. Its function is that of giving the individuals the capacity to respond in the face of aggression against their own territory, or at least to what our brain considers as our own.

For Sun Tzu, territory is the foundation of the State and despite too much Western legislation with too many laws going against common sense (that is, biological laws!) with the ability to throw you in prison (because you hurt or killed that guy who entered your home with malicious intentions and without being invited...), I'm sure that for the majority of you, the right of self-defense is something unquestionable. But let's leave aside the generalized softening of our societies when dealing with this issue (something that would for many involve more than one editorial!). Violence not only has that defensive function, it has possesses the function of offering us the ability to attack in order to reach our objectives and cover our needs. "The possibility of victory resides in the attack," affirms Sun Tzu. Without what is today that so reviled violence, humans would have been devoured by lice, or any other bug of the many that crawled around the planet at that time looking at us while they salivated like someone looking at his dinner. And that without counting the "friends" of our own species.

This way of looking at violence as something bad is only one more sign of the decrepitude of our modern societies in which the natural principles have been displaced by human laws and good intentions to the point of absurdity. No, it doesn't seem to me that such a thing has been a bad idea; to put this matter in order is essential so that our lives can unfold in a civilized fashion; however, it bothers me that the "well-thinking" and the exuding of stupidity with which the social spokespersons encourage the masses to see everything that smells of violence as a cancer that must be removed. People, there is no coin that doesn't have another side! And to try to negate violence is the best way to castrate ourselves as a collective. Violence is a natural instinct and since man has been man, he has had to live with it (and survive thanks to it!), putting it at the service of the species, of the group or of the individual, and of his objectives. The Martial Arts are a magnificent way of channeling, in a civilized fashion, a reality that is wholly unquestionable, re-directing a force whose utility continues, and will continue, to be basic and fundamental for each one of us.

If we observe the essential functions of violence, we understand that once it has served us for defending and occupying territory considered as our own, for providing us with what is necessary like food and water, its most immediate function is that of facilitating our reproduction and the perpetuation of the species: it is here where the force of Venus makes its theatrical entrance, full of charms and promises of pleasure.

Probably our ancestors behaved more like their cousins, the rest of the mammals, challenging other males in order to attain the privilege of mating with the females. Such prerogative survived in Europe even to the Middle Ages in the famous "privilege rights" of the feudal lords and in one way or another we can find residuals of such customs even in our days.

The very sexual act is charged with symbolism and violent components: we "eat" our partners, we smell them, lick them, penetrate their bodily territory, we hold, squeeze, etc.... And what can you tell me about the sighs and groans that often accompany the most exalted executioners of the art of love-making? They seem like the grunts in a fight. Even in their modern and civilized version—that is, with consent—sexual relationships have all the components of Mars that you care to find, to say nothing about fetishes...

Sex is the promise of pleasure with which nature forces us to follow through with its plans of perpetuation. Venus, the god of love who is born from the sperm of Uranus when his son Saturn castrates him, has some very violent sisters, the furies. Part of the sperm of Uranus (the primordial god of the heavens that each night rapes the earth god, mother of Saturn) fell into the foam of the sea from where Venus was born, but from the part of the sperm that fell on land, the three furies were born. Venus, then, is a polarization of the essential force of the heavens, that which took the part from the lion, while her sisters are not what one would call the most attractive gods. Venus is the stimulus of the promise of achievement, the sweet present of pleasure, relief from pain and its opposite side, plentitude of bliss and seduction; it is the hidden side of Mars, mysterious like his eighth superior, the also aquatic Neptune, and even more solvent than her. Venus comforts and recompenses what is gotten my Mars, one the stick, the other the carrot with which nature humbles kings and tribunes, rich and poor, big and small.

Sex and violence always appear in our stories and mythologies, inseparably united and continuously present in our lives. To understand their nature is an essential aspect of human development and to try to ignore their power is to put into the hands of others the politics of its use as natural and powerful forces that are in our lives. Religions, cultures, and states have always attempted to organize (with unequal success...) human thought in these two matters, conscious of the power they possess. The warrior, as a challenger of his own ignorance, must give them his full attention, make them priority matters in his life, confronting with sincerity and with no limit but his own impeccability, all their facets and powers, exploring through his feelings and experiences where his measure is fulfilled, where his necessities are reduced.

Violence and Sex: I already know that, as always, my way is a general discourse, that I don't very much like going into details. Not much space? Or perhaps that is my prerogative? Good heavens! Everyone does what he likes! But if you ask me my opinion, if you ask me what I advise, a formula that will work in these matters... I wouldn't know what to tell you... All formulas, if they are not paradoxical, are partial and incomplete and wind up provoking that which they try to avoid, and far from me is that chalice! However, and to offer some reply, it seems to me that a good measure of practicality could be reduced to a simple phrase that everyone understands: "Don't do to others what you wouldn't want them to do to you," except, of course, if they ask you to...

"Sex is the promise of pleasure with which nature forces us to follow through with its plans of perpetuation"

THE WAY OF MORIHEI
A trip to the interior
Of the genius creator of Aikido

When one reads the texts of Ueshiba, one perceives how behind them there lies a strong spiritual disposition that probably many martial artists have not known how to value properly. Some for excessive piousness and prosody, the mystics, others for defect, the lovers of the punch, but the case is that in the end this aspect of the Grand Master Morihei Ueshiba has found unequal eco among his heirs.

It's sure that Ueshiba has a stormy biography, to put it mildly, and that his life is plagued with episodes and relationships of the most extravagant kinds. Ueshiba wasn't a run-of-the-mill man, and like all geniuses, he possessed and was possessed by a character full of deficiencies. But it was precisely thanks to these and to his effort to overcome himself and reach a certain inner peace that he managed to create such a peculiar formulation of combat. However, the achievements of Ueshiba are not so much in the forms, undoubtedly debtors to a great extent to a very rich martial tradition, studied at length by many experts (Takeda, etc.). It is in his drawing together of the very concept of the meeting of two forces, in his search to find a wholly satisfactory response that is always in accord with the Universal Order where Ueshiba was revolutionary.

The "loving Budo" Background and contemporary philosophies

It is said that Ueshiba in his youth was an excessively impetuous man and of course his first technical formulations are not very different from much of the old Japanese schools. The differentiating jump is probably related to an internal jump, the result of a posterior change in his relationship with Omoto and his trip to China. Many have wanted to see in that trip transforming contacts with local Masters, but I consider this idea unlikely. The Japanese, despite their proverbial admiration for the Chinese culture, were not, let's say, very given over to mixing. The most logical thing is to think that it was a transformation stemming from his personal experiences on that trip which began to define a crisis of values that led him to his Aikido.

It is not the first case in history of a martial Master re-converted, to put it one way, into a man of knowledge. Miyamoto Musashi was a noteworthy precedent, of course, but the cases are much more frequent than it seems. Boredom and distancing from violence after a life of confrontations, coincide with a spiritual awakening, a Satori, in which the subject perceives the invisible Unity among all things and the laws that govern it.

The principal philosophical characteristic of Ueshiba is the superimposition of the unifying principle on the principle of dispersion. Ueshiba calls his Budo, "Loving Budo". Of course, this expression mustn't be understood in a simplistic or gullible way. Love is the force, the universal principle of attraction, and in its extreme, the fusion of the polar forces, while war is the principle of repulsion, not in the sense of aversion, loathing, or antipathy (though also, of course), rather even in its more simple physical form: the repulsion of two poles with the same charge, the same charge that not only impedes them from fusing, but that stimulates and drives their separation.

The two opposite and complementary principles are present in traditional culture, in the animism and philosophies of the Far East, in a way that they were an inseparable part of the intellectual formation of any Master of the time. Yin and Yang, In and Yo, in Japanese, symbolize the forces that manifest this plane of reality dominated by duality. The unifying principle was established (or recovered if one notes the multiple traditions of Taoist roots) by numerous personalities of great intellectual influence in the same years and places in which Ueshiba applied his findings to Budo. Of course, Nyoti Sakurazawa Oshawa, the creator of Macrobiotics, was not the least of them, a man who established the relationships between the polar forces in a philosophy, which is, I'm afraid, as in the case with Ueshiba, little understood.

For example, Ueshiba never hid his relationships with the Omoto sect, a group that undoubtedly dealt with esoteric concepts connected to animism and Japanese Shinto. In such beliefs and practices, both principles and concepts are continually present in the form of deities, demons, or elemental forces. Such a relationship and antecedents don't detract from nor diminish in any way the discovery of Ueshiba; however, it is convenient in order to understand it adequately, to put the Master in the context of his time and place in order to value the origin and the interdependences that allowed for the rapid acceptance and diffusion of formulations like his in those years.

The unifying principle is present in Chinese literature, principally in the Taoist texts of Lao Tzu and Chuang Tzu, two authentic geniuses when it comes to establishing the principles of nature. In them, the reference to water as the symbol of infinite adaptation, fluidity, and constant change appears reiterated, an image that Aikido adopted with force. Nature as the first and ultimate truth, as the only unmistaken and infallible Master, is another image that Ueshiba repeated with frequency. But without a doubt, Taoism contributes as a precedent above all other things the idea of unity, of Ai, union, graphics that illustrate this text from the hand of the O Sensei himself.

The Unifying Principle of the "Uni-verse"

For Ueshiba, the unifying principle is the highest of the strategies since it transcends difference by integrating. But how does one apply it precisely to combat, something essentially dominated by the disintegrating force, war?

Kano established the principle of flexibility, of softness, observing leaves on bamboo stems while retired in the Nanzenji monastery, how they yielded under the weight of the snow. The survival linked to flexibility indicated a formula that Kano established: **"If they push you, yield; if they pull you, advance,"** a concept that Ueshiba took to its ultimate consequences: **"If they push you, absorb their force and make it turn around you."**

In the practice of Ueshiba's Aikido, it was the adaptation of the principle of unification against that of disintegration. The atemis were not eliminated but their use is not that of an attack in the true sense of the word, and it was minimized. The opponent frequently "hit himself" against the fist instead of the fist itself hitting... each step was the natural consequence of the tone and intensity of the adversary's attack, a continuous adaptation to his forms that took advantage of all his force to channel it from a center that was not only geometric but energetic.

Tying the center to the very earth is not a simple exercise in visualization. Many styles work with that concept, but there's no doubt that in Ueshiba, such an idea was conceived in order to be applied. Tori in Aikido must be capable of making the opponent turn in a spiral around his center. For that, the greatest firmness of the very center is sine que non compulsory. For that, he determined:

"Make your heart the heart of the very universe."

The Uni-verse, literally, **"the One in movement"**, seems, then, a concept inseparable from Ueshiba's conception.

"Budo is a way with heart," states the classic saying, Budo, not kokoro. It is the identification with the only beginning, a non-transferable experience, what makes the act of the warrior making himself the center possible, emptying himself of emotion or intention.

But Ueshiba warns the mystics:

"Don't think that the divine is above us. It's here, inside us and around us. The aim of Aikido is to remind us that we are in a state of grace."

The grace arises from the internal realization of the ultimate truth, the principle of unity. One doesn't reach it by the techniques, as some would hope, rather, the correct techniques are the result of such a realization. The initiate, raising the plane of his consciousness, realizes unity and therefore can't attack himself nor be defeated by himself.

For Ueshiba, said Unity is taken to its maximum consequences:

"In the true Budo, there are no opponents. In the true Budo we seek to be One with all things, to return to the heart of creation."

The knowledge in Ueshiba arises from the direct comprehension of the laws, which, though hidden from the sight of the profane, are continually in front of our eyes:

"The universe is our greatest Master, our greatest friend... the Universe itself is always teaching us Aikido but we don't know how to perceive it."

"The true Budo is an application of love. The path of a warrior is not to destroy and kill, but to feed life, to continually create. Love is the divinity that can truly protect us."

The equalization of these principles in specific techniques is not the real raison d'étre of Aikido such as its creator conceived it, however, the majority of its students are not capable of seeing this simple question. This dissociation is because the success of the very technical formulation of the Art of O Sensei was at such a level (something always much more understandable than the concepts that underlie it), that Aikido has been winning over followers exponentially in the past decades.

Fission and fusion, a synchronic jump in the consciousness of humanity

Re-reading Ueshiba, I don't believe that he was a mystic; more like a "touched" man of action, that much, yes, touched by great inner torment, real anxiousness, and of knowledge almost incomparable. The Aikido born from his own inner voyage was not a success due to his training, but what gave expression to a personal conquest, of an internal discovery and contrary to other visionaries, prophets and men of knowledge, it isn't derived from a divine revelation since the concept of a personalized god doesn't exist in the Oriental culture. It is the principle of one, the unity of all things that exists arising in each moment from the emptiness that occupies such a place.

The unifying concept in the Martial Arts and in many other activities of the human being is contemporary with the first atomic explosion. Nuclear fission appears synchronic to the concept of universal fusion. Like a game of Yin and Yang, it isn't a coincidence that in the same place where this took place for the first time, Japan, it was the mother country of people like Ueshiba who have bequeathed on us magnificent examples of the jump in the consciousness of the planet that supposes an understanding and application of the concept to something concrete, the understanding that everything is One.

Ueshiba was, like all of us, a product of his time and of his nature, but his legacy, the quintessence of his experience, have transcended him and continues awakening many people years after his death. A discovery, a conquest, that has undoubtedly placed him among the greatest martial artists of all time.

UNITY.
THE MARTIAL ARTS
ON A COMMON FRONT

*"When we make the adversary our objective
we ourselves become the enemy."*

All is One and manifests itself differentiated, so reads the first law of the Universe. The principle of unity isn't separate from the martial philosophies and their culture, however, its practical application in our collective is still a dream today. The Martial Arts form a group of titanic proportions if taken together. Separately, even the biggest organizations poorly compete with any other mass activity. On the other hand, the differentiation generates an unquestionable wealth in form and content. Now that the singular way of thinking and the globalization rolling pin put everything under their crushing politics on equal terms (to equate by the minimums), discoving that in our profession no year passes in which styles (new or traditional) of great interest flower never ceases to be magnificent news.

The MA are alive, they regenerate themselves, interact, combine, stimulate, and contrast. Even the competition between styles hasn't stopped being a healthy stimulus, while we won't forget that we all navigate on a common ship, and that it isn't at the cost of our neighbor that our style will grow and attain greater diffusion, but for the adequate display and demonstration of its virtues, for work well done, honest and generous. But when we make the adversary our objective, we ourselves become the enemy.

Fortunately, they are less and less, but there are still dinosaurs that practice the old politics of attacking other styles, of looking down on them, of making their lives as impossible as they are able to. This is a stupid attitude, like that of throwing stones at one's own house, but they, in their small-time mentality, or in their exclusive fundamentalism, shield themselves in old prerogatives empty of any real value in order to undertake their misdeeds. Of course, these pathetic individuals no longer train, taking cover behind their institutionalized armchairs, sitting on their fat butts to put all their energy at the service of no other interest except that of staying at the front of their little kingdom of factions, controlling, for the most part, money that is not theirs.

For the society, the MA are a big unknown. There is no culture to this respect beyond the films of Bruce Lee and the Kung Fu series. Not even the martial sports have yet achieved the preeminence that they deserve in the sports media, both newspaper and television. All kinds of combat, whether considered Art or not, form an amorphous and undifferentiated whole in the heads of the majority of the citizens, be they Korean, Japanese, Chinese, or Malaysian. This is admirable activity for the power that it bestows on its practitioners compared to the laymen in the matter, but also a matter capable of immediately generating an easy joke. For the society in general, we martial artists are all curious and exotic individuals, when not dangerous, since our prime material is violence, and that is something that disturbs and upsets those who, instead of confronting it and re-channeling it positively as we ourselves do in our practices, deny it like an ostrich hiding its head when facing fear.

For that, every time that I hear these myopic good-for-nothings pleased with the problems of the martial neighbor, my blood boils. What these short-sighted boneheads don't know is that sooner or later they might well be on the same list. The saying goes, "those who live by the sword, die by the sword" and though their exclusivisms don't allow them to see it, the problems of their "neighbors" are their problems.

In the zoology of the exclusivists, there are all kinds of awful things, but I don't want to leave out that of evoking what simply acts as the truck farmer's dog (which neither eats the cabbage nor lets the master eat it). Jealous of the success of others, they dedicate themselves to conspire from their little spaces of power, instead of trying to look at themselves in order to understand where they are mistaken, and in this way undertake measures to improve and learn from their errors. They have lost all the nobility that the way of the warrior confers to fall into the dark side of the force and they don't deserve to form a part of something so beautiful.

Unity confers sense and direction, power and influence; dispersion only brings chaos. For any true martial artist, the "other" styles are at least an object of curiosity. One does what one does because he or she likes it, or because that option and not another simply crosses one's path, but since we only love what we know, we learn to appreciate the virtues of our practice. This has its positive side to the extent that it allows us to go deeply into our own styles and all the styles together comprise a rich gathering of knowledge that require a lot of time and effort in order to be dominated and integrated. However, we can't, with the nobility and respect that we learn on the tatamis, deny the value of the other forms of combat only because they aren't ours. I think that the practitioners, knowing what it takes to learn any style by personal experience, are always much more respectful than the politicians. I am convinced that that sense of unity exists much more at the bases than in the upper echelons, more on the tatamis than in the offices, in the hearts than in the pockets, and sooner or later those who do not follow the right path will pay for it.

Integrating is a greater strategy than that of discriminating; it's certain that difference must exist and be carefully cultivated to its extreme, and that is nothing else but individuality, but it's no less important that we can't lose the North. The martial family is one. It drinks from the same roots and these are not in any geographical place, rather in the heart and in the nature of man and the world.

While there is a man who gets up, like Prometheus, to try to steal the fire of wisdom from the gods, there will be warriors in the world. While there are those who vibrate facing the power of nature and who want to walk through the world with the gallantry and honor of one who fights to possess himself, there will be martial artists. But if we aren't capable of uniting our forces, and of understanding that though more or less separated in the forms, we are all one big family, our enemies, those who look at us with distrust for daring to be warriors, those who to keep us quiet, to castrate and control us in a thousand different ways, will be able to, first, shut us up, and second, dominate us, and finally, end our noble practices.

Let such a thing never happen! We begin, then, from today, looking to our martial brothers for what they are, cultivating this camaraderie and respect, this mutual collaboration that the great Jigoro Kano ordered us to do (if he raised his head!), by maintaining unity of action, the battle will be ours. Let it be this way!

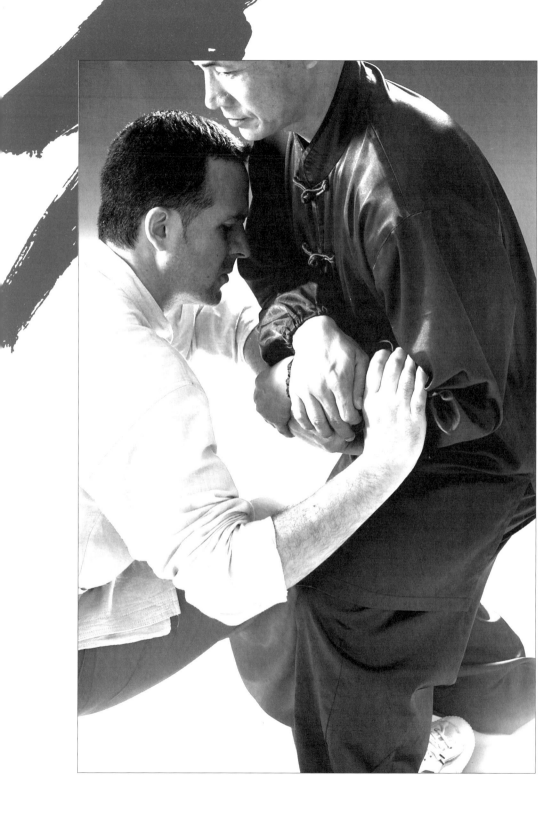

A LOT OF EFFICIENCY...
FEW PRACTITIONERS

"The greatest efficiency in combat resides in avoiding it."
The Art of War, Sun Tsu

To be or to practice an efficient Martial Art is one of the values in vogue in the past years. When one says efficiency, it seems as though any combative formula is justified and any style that doesn't raise this flag is not legitimate. But efficiency in and of itself is no more than a horizon toward which we can or cannot walk, according to what we feel our journey must be. Efficiency in the ring, with rules or without rules, isn't the same as in the street; with arms as without them; with legal limitations as a law enforcement agent or fighting for your life... in the battle field, or on a street corner in your neighborhood. So, speaking about efficiency is speaking about everything... and nothing. Efficiency has become an empty word, hackneyed, a sale's slogan, an everything full of many "nothings".

The styles that are the fruit of the revolution of Free Fight have wanted to appropriate this principle staging combats in circumstances where the pre-eminence of its specialization has become irrefutable. The marketing campaign that they have put in motion and enjoy today is spectacular, receiving attention in the media that perhaps only JKD had previously, an Art that promulgated similar objectives, curiously with similar results: a lot of press, few practitioners.

Beyond the initial surprise at the appearance of these styles, the final impact on the number of practitioners hasn't been so noticeable, and I'd even go further, not even worth mentioning. Why does this divorce between both factors exist? The question has a simple answer: efficiency isn't the principle factor that practitioners consider when it comes to choosing one style or another. As much as this might leave some perplexed, there is no better explanation and the professionals in the matter would be better off taking note of it.

In modern Western societies, especially among the more economically comfortable populations, this idea of going around knocking one another on the ground doesn't seem like the best way to pass the time. In everyone's omnipotent fantasies there might exist the inherent idea of pleasure at striking another, but what doesn't fit into such a daydream is the sad confrontation with reality when you discover later that the other one can do the same to you, and that even in the best of cases, when that doesn't happen, it is very probable that in your feat you break your hand and spend three months unable to work and bored, without even being able to chat on the internet.

The good combatants and fighters always come from poor countries, where for some, the only way to move up the social ladder is perhaps by hitting. However, there is a strong desire to practice martial formulas all around the planet, including in the first world, and this must find its course. What, then, takes precedent in the method of selection?

There are patterns in everything, contextual factors such the proximity of the gymnasium, that friend who encourages you, the price, etc. They are not insignificant, of course; but we mustn't forget others like good marketing, correct systemization, and the most important of all, satisfying the needs and expectations of your client. And it's because we live in a consumer society and your combat style is a product. As consumers, we choose from among distinct offers and effectiveness is only one more parameter, it is not "the parameter" that many believe it to be. The mixed Martial Arts, despite their success in the rings, continue to be a miniscule percentage of the total number of practitioners and, of course, they are very far from the incredible figures of Karate or Taekwondo. It's certain that many of these practitioners like to participate as spectators at Boxing, K-1, or Vale Tudo events, but they have it very clear that they are not up to training these martial formulas themselves. They simply don't offer what they are looking for, they don't satisfy their necessities.

Curiously, much of what the MMA have looked down on are essential elements when it comes to choosing, and the cultural and sociological values connected to these traditional practices are not the least of their charm. The capacity to limit the damage to oneself and others, not only in confrontation but also in the practice itself, are other values to highlight. I would even say that their therapeutic capacities and the extent to which they offer improved health and psychological well-being move up in the ranking of the reasons that push us to make decisions, not only when it comes to choosing one Art or another, but especially when it comes to continuing its practice once past a certain age, and we can't forget that modern societies are growing old!

The omnipotent dream is a predominantly adolescent fantasy. The values of maturity are others and this counts a lot when it comes to beginning; when the ones who choose are mommy and daddy, who are the ones who pay the bills, it is their values that prevail, and normally to them, in these times of few children, they can tend toward a natural protectionism. They already have enough accepting the piercings, tattoos, ethnicities, and other apparently counter-cultural fashions—on the other hand so proper of the Free Fighter iconography—to consider their little ones risking themselves physically doing idiotic things on a tatami.

There are educational and formative values that have a lot of power and weight. There are benefits that aren't very apparent but that offer great returns for those who put on a kimono, dobok, Hakama, etc., training with diligence two or three times a week without any desire at all of winning a championship, or of becoming the first cousin of "Hulk". They train because they feel better, because they enjoy learning to coordinate their bodies, to liberate tension in a controlled and acceptable way with low risk; to find a certain peace that they didn't have before, a certain tempering, something approaching serenity, an extra stimulus for self-confidence, and even a sense of belonging to a group from which sometimes the most peculiar friends arise with whom you have shared effort at times, and a beer other times.

The simple values of the average practitioner are those that have made Martial Arts great in our modern societies, and in the intoxication of the media success, the ones who are betting on the most muscular horse shouldn't forget that; perhaps we are repeating the story of David and Goliath and in the end, the one who wins is simply... good with his hands.

CONCENTRATION AND MEDITATION IN MARTIAL ARTS

Concentration and meditation are inseparable acts, joined to the traditional practices of Martial Arts. However, there are very few people who comprehend the meaning and the necessity of its practice.

Neophytes (and not so neophytes!) wonder about the meditation during classes. As they always repeat the action that they see the Master do, and as this really doesn't have any visible element, they find themselves disconcerted facing this disquieting silence, facing an inexplicable situation in which there are no directions. Is this a waste of time? What is it that one is supposed to do during those moments? What must we think about? What is the meaning of such practices?

To these and other questions I hope to respond in this article.

Meditation frequently takes place at the end and at the beginning of classes. However, the very fact of arriving at the Dojo, freeing oneself of our street clothes to put on our Gui, Dobok, or whatever is worn, and adjusting our belt is in itself an act of preparation to adapt our mind to that other space-time that makes up our practice in the Do-jo (the place of awakening).

Meditation and the initial greetings are one more step in this aforementioned process. Even in its exclusively formal practice, said ceremonies facilitate the transition from the hectic day-to-day state to a distinct attitude where values, time, and even the measure of our effort are very different. Here, money doesn't control everything, the Master controls everything; our time doesn't belong to us, it is managed by the Master and the group dynamic; the body, frequently left aside during the day, now takes on a distinct role, is made present, and calls the mind and the emotions to participate in the effort. An effort that one does not make to get money, or objects, or sex, it is a force that will only bring one gift: overcoming the self. Such a change is not trivial and requires a process of adaptation, a kind of "hyperbaric chamber" of the soul in order for one not to "explode" in the transition.

The Dojo was traditionally a sacred place. In reality, the Dojo is the external expression of an interior state that we must acquire stopping our world, detaining the inner dialogue. What makes the Dojo sacred is penetrating ourselves, getting into a sacred state through the abandonment of our daily thinking, of our worries, problems, obsessions, of the run-run of our tyrannical minds, always incapable of ceasing to move from here to there.

Conscious of these nuances, the old Masters provided a ceremony that would put us in a position to make the change in order, in this way, to get the full attention of their followers during the learning process.

The true Eastern Masters teach a lot more from silence than the Westerners. This is for two reasons. The first is that the Eastern culture is more self-controlled, and the second is that the objective of their teaching is frequently not focused on what is visible. In such a framework, reason is not a practical tool, rather it is usually a nuisance for the evolution of the neophyte. We Westerners verbalize everything without stopping and in this way our minds never cease to work. The silence of meditation can be something more than uncomforting for someone who comes to a traditional class for the first time. Silence can even create anxiety, such is the limitation of our capacity.

Meditation is an act of emptying, not of filling up. It is not about thinking about this or that, it is simply about leaving thinking aside. At the beginning, this is something incomprehensible for anyone lacking experience. They have educated our minds since our birth to be a tool that continually works in order to get things; don't think that changing this routine is something easy to do.

The idea of the emptiness that all things contain is a very Eastern concept and comes from Taoist philosophy. Essentially, to access that emptiness is to come into contract with the fundamental and eternal that exists in all things. For that, we must free our attention from distractions. For this, many schools have developed concentration techniques based on redirecting attention to the most essential act that we do automatically, to the act that allows us to live every second: breathing. These techniques are not insignificant and will help the beginner to find initial support. However, this doesn't mean that it ceases to be an act, a doing, when the essence of meditation is precisely that of "non-action." This "non-action" must be, nonetheless, conscious. It is not about sleeping, something that is more than common at the beginning if the practice goes on too long. "The action of non-action," the "wu-wei" of the Chinese, is closer to the unattached observation of ourselves. Don't resist the "run-run" of your thoughts because any effort in that direction will probably create the opposite effect. Let them fly and pass by you as if it were a kind of mental voyeurism. Don't stop the thoughts, but neither should you get stuck on any of them; let the mind jump from one to the other, like background noise, while you feel how the air enters and exits from the lungs through the nose. You shouldn't even identify with the object that breathes, do it with the air, with each breath coming and going with the flow and re-flow of the tide of life, beyond, where there is only silence and quietude.

The habitual thing in meditation is to practice it in the lotus or diamond (Seiza) posture. The only indispensable thing is to maintain the spine erect and perpendicular to the floor. If your back bothers you, see an osteopath. At least the meditation will have served to help you notice something!

The idea of the position for meditation is simply to achieve the maximum relaxation possible. Adapting the body to these postures to which we are not accustomed can take time. In Seiza, the feet can bother you and if our circulation is not good, we can feel like they are asleep and it can even hurt. In the lotus posture, or half lotus, it is the knees that can complain, or simply that we can't even do it at all.

Once these inconveniences are overcome, we must, as a first stage, practice conscious relaxation, paying attention to areas throughout the whole body. It helps to follow some kind of order so as not to leave anything out of the exercise. The objective is to reach a state of tranquility and relaxation without losing tone and attention. The eyes, half-open or closed, depending on the school, must "look without seeing."

There are primarily two areas where we can direct our attention in this first phase, the hara, or tan-tien, and the pineal gland (third eye). In the first case, the eyes look roughly two meters to the floor in front of us. In the second, they are, while closed, raised to the spot between the eye-brows. Zen meditation, which is what is normally practiced in the Dojos, places attention on the tan-tien, and not in vain its objective is to prepare us for a practice in which said point must be the anchorage and starting point of our action. The hands repose on the thighs without resting on the abdomen. With the palms upward, the thumbs barely touch one another, closing the energetic circle. "Neither valley nor mountain," states the Zen saying, the thumbs are extended and reposed but still with tone, not just floppy.

There are an infinity of concentration and meditation techniques, but we can't ever forget what the strategic objective of the practice is. To lose oneself in the details of the techniques is another way of treating your practice like an object and therefore of losing ourselves again in the branches that impede our seeing the forest.

The Martial Arts are meditation in movement, however, at the beginning, and especially at the end of the classes, once the tensions are freed up and the energy channels are open, the execution of the meditation offers the practitioner a unique chance to de-accelerate, temper and calm the agitation, get perspective, slow down the rhythm and access a genuine and lasting state of peace.

Ignoring this discipline during training, as I see happening more and more in the gymnasiums, is the result of the acceleration and anxiety that our modern way of life produces. Though at first imperceptible, the time invested in meditation pays for itself many times over, favoring the growth and the assimilation of all the implicit good that exists in Martial practice. It improves attention in class and as time goes on we can access that acquired mental state faster and faster in order to give over the attention of all of our five senses.

The transition toward an alert but tempered state of consciousness is an uncommon achievement for a human being. The bad thing is that at arriving there, they don't give you any medals or prizes or something you can hang up, nothing that can justify it in the purely pragmatic perspective, that which we have all been fervently educated. However, the immaterial achievements of this training have a much broader influence in what is even more important to us in the world, our well-being. But it is already known, the refrain says it: "There is no shortcut without work." And it seems that the practice of the "useless" can paradoxically become the useful.

If the Martial Arts were not a door to the transformation of consciousness, they would be reduced to physical practices of skills that are almost always useless, since in the end, how often do we have to hit someone in life? And yet, each day, each second, we have no other option than to "co-exist" with that anxious, stressed, and frustrated person, the one who has to pay bills, win the respect and affection of others, carry out our necessities, and on top of that know that we have an expiration date! For that person who we see every morning when we look at ourselves in the mirror, couldn't we invest a little time, some minutes to him? In the end, he hasn't stopped being a good boy, though everything got complicated for him… Let's throw him a rope!

"If the Martial Arts were not a door to the transformation of consciousness, they would be reduced to physical practices of skills that are almost always useless"

FANATICISM

When the group of bobbies from Scotland Yard discovered that the suicide bombers in London hadn't been born in Palestine, Riyadh, or Mesopotamia, but in the very heart of the "Empire," they must have had faces of perplexity worthy of passing into history. The same face of incredulity that we saw in the television interviews with the terrorists' neighbors days afterward.

Mixed societies have great advantages, but also enormous inconveniences. The days following the attack, as was foreseeable, it wasn't easy to contain the hooligans. How do you explain to someone like that that it isn't the same to be Muslim as it is to be radical. The hooligan is a man of simple criteria; what he sees is that the guy who presses the button and who, coincidently, practices the same faith and beliefs as those terrorists who attacked Madrid or New York. However, the hooligan doesn't know that he is accused of the same tendency, of the same radicalizing force that indifferently encourages and pushes those young people to go into the subway with a bomb attached to their bodies: that force is fanaticism.

Fanaticism is a kind of intellectual blindness not easily cured. It is founded on negative and rancid emotion that invades the natural space of jurisdiction of the mind. The person no longer reflects, rather repeats a loop, a closed circuit of thoughts that give known feedback. Without external references, without contrast, it is impossible to have one's own criteria.

The world doesn't stop being a description, an entelechy of nature where horror is seen daily. In our "gray" societies, the ranges are reduced and they are turning more and more each day toward black and white. With each step toward the extremes, the coloring and amplitude diminish; with each new tension, we draw closer to the abyss of the extremes of radicalization worthy of our Kali Yuga.

Our Western society is in crisis, but: Are the values and ideals under which we have lived capable of providing the firmness and the flexibility necessary to defeat this new enemy? It seems that the aphorism "adapt or die" is now true more than ever, and it is no longer valid to merely condemn terrorism or lament what has happened; it is necessary to understand that we must learn from errors and establish the measures to change the paradigm that makes possible the very existence of the enemy and their capacity to act with impunity. However, sometimes the mute, other times the amplifications of the media, and especially the spokespersons of "good intentions" send us to a recreated and manipulated reality where the very idea of reaction is confusing. Sympathetic or parasympathetic? Forward or backward? We seem to be aground in no man's land, without an answer to the questions: Where is the unacceptable? What is the limit? What is the price we are willing to pay?

In my humble opinion, things will have to get a lot worse for there to be a reaction really proportional to the push received since 9-11. It seems that we are capable of adapting ourselves so much that a greater reaction requires a much greater affront. In the end, we have learned to co-exist with many more deaths, for example, on the highways, though we consider that an acceptable price for our freedom of using the car. To what point are we going to be capable of compromising our way of life, our freedoms, in order to act against this adversary?

The tactics of terrorism have always been that of wear and tear. When you can't defeat a superior enemy, you don't confront it frontally; the only solution is undermine their morale and to hit them where it most hurts, in order to eventually force them to yield, or if that's not possible, negotiate strategic objectives, generally territorial. However, this new way of globalized terrorism doesn't seem to be pursuing territories (but, in the end, that, too!). More than anything, it concerns itself with and proposes a new paradigm based on a particular reading of the Koran's sacred scriptures, and their enemy is the "unfaithful," that is, and not to go on about it: all that does not agree with their perception of the world.

The term "fanatic" comes from the Latin "fanaticus" and from its root, "fanum," which means temple. There's no doubt: the wise fathers of our culture already knew back then about the intrinsic relationship existent between both things, and it is clear that man, despite all of our technology, has not changed so much.

On the other hand, Westerners, always so subtle and shrewd, established, millenniums ago, through the Go Kyo, the five elements, some keys that could shed certain light on this question. The fanatic, from this viewpoint, is undoubtedly a being dominated by negative Fire energy. Curiously, the lamb is fire energy and the Middle East the place with the greatest "wood" energy, this element—wood—being the precedent and the mother of Fire. The lamb-eating populations would be prone to fire energy since, in the end, we are nothing more than the product of the environment, and food is not the least of these conditioners. In the same way, the pork-eating populations, such as the Chinese, nourished on an animal with water energy, have always been dominated by this force; in the same way, those of cow, earth energy, etc., etc.

The culture medium of discontent is spreading through the peripheral neighborhoods of the big European and American urban areas; on the other hand, it has always been so. In the pyramid that society defines, there always have to be more bricks below supporting those above, if not, and if the flow of those who enter from below finds that there is little "porosity" for them to eventually rise up, they get mad, and it confuses them. The optimists believe that they can "fix" society and eliminate the "injustices" so that we can all be equal. Some, imbued with such "good intentions," left behind them an enormous holocaust. But nature loathes equality; nature is and will be hierarchical, and the pyramid with its number pi is not in vain, and for that, the symbol of perfection in our scheme of things. From Egypt to the dollar bill, from Tenochtitlan to social graphs, the pyramid sends a silent message, a message as ancient as it is everlasting. Do you hear it?

The "fanaticus" have come out of their "fanum" in order to impose their vision of the world. We can ask ourselves anything you want, what ours is, or to what point we are willing to go to defend it; even whether you want to defend it or not! But meanwhile, don't think that they are going to reduce their lethal and fanatical activities by themselves, or because some god comes down from the heavens and convinces them to do so. Nor will they abandon it because they eventually get their "justice." Those people who set off the bombs on the subways, buses, and trains didn't have it so bad, certainly infinitely better than those in Ethiopia or Nigeria. When we forget that we belong to that 5% of the privileged world population that eats three times a day, we realize the universal truth that everything is relative.

We live in times of extremism, of the radicalization of forces. The Martial Arts (in which there are also negative fanatics!), were made to forge warriors, externally and internally. Never before in history has there been so much demand for both. But most of all, never before has there existed so much necessity of focused warriors who act like a silent chain of good sense, firmness, and of that objectivity that can only arise from someone who dominates him or herself. Now, one can't work one's center when from the exterior, from the periphery, people walk around planting bombs; perhaps it is necessary to go out and do something... though it only be so they leave one in peace with his own and true war, that which we all fight against ourselves.

"...never before has there existed so much necessity of focused warriors who act like a silent chain of good sense, firmness, and of that objectivity that can only arise from someone who dominates him or herself"

THE MARTIAL ARTS AT THE CROSSROADS

"We are like a drop of water in the sea.
When we join with it,
we participate in the whole that we never ceased being"

The conglomeration that we call the "World of Martial Arts" is a whole with its own entity, very much despite those who insist on seeing the world with a microscope, putting the accent on the differences, as if these were really something substantial and separate. It sounds strange, this re-occurring distinction in times in which we already know that the human genome is distinguished from the fruit fly's by only a miniscule percentage... What we have here is a lot of soaking egos (that's how they bloat) and a lot of nonsense!

That Budo is One and proceeds from one essential origin is unquestionable. Wanting to magnify what separates us is more a marketing tactic than a scientific assertion. No. I won't bore you with theories about a possible common historical origin. For me, there are hardcore truths that precede these digressions and these underlie the very nature of what is Martial. Man, since he has been man, confronted his position, both in the world and in nature, through fighting. Budo is only the result of this effort and the conquests facing said difficulty. With all its cultural, racial, and environmental particulars, the path of the warrior possesses in its essence a common point of origin, that of responding to some unquestionable necessities that are common to all of us as a species. Later we can talk about any point concerning this theme that we want, but the way of the warrior took place there where there was a man, and in the end all of us participate in its essence... the rest is, in the best of cases, culture, and in the worst... just self-importance.

The martial variety is a treasure, surely, but trying to give preponderance to the differences about that which is not common is like trying to put up doors in the countryside. When some people who I considered intelligent insist on following these lines of thinking, I have no choice but to lower my consideration of them to that of sectarians.

Unfortunately, I discover all too frequently these tendencies exclusive to our sector. There is a kind of hick-like "provincialism", of small-minded militancy in which the trees don't allow them to see the forest. And you will say, So what? Well, that's very bad, my friends, very bad indeed, because separately we are something miniscule, socially insignificant, and yet, together we would be an influential and active group in the society. For the "non-practitioners", we are all more or less in the same bag. No, this is not soccer, or tennis, or even is it something reducible to the simple sphere of the sportive. Budo, Martial Arts, is a much bigger conglomeration but inclusive in its breadth and approaches, in what is offered, but insignificant from style to style compared to all those sports for the masses. Who is guilty of this? Let's look at the naval... Yes, what I do is only sport; yes, what I do is different, it is an Art! Yes, mine is an inner path; mine is Olympic and yours isn't; mine is... Yours is nothing without the others, man! But together we would be something else!

In the magazine circles, a good gage as model of the entire sector, it is a proven fact that all those adventures with a more sectarian idea that have been initiated or planned in the past 40 years in Europe and America have failed, or if they have survived, they have done so symbolically, almost always with low circulation. It is lamentable to observe the perpetuation of the blindness that can be seen in our sector.

The world is living times of radicalization. The force goes to the extremes in all fields, and in the Martial Arts also. On one side there are the forces with unifying tendencies. Some forces whose perfect summary and metaphor we can find in that phrase of the immortals, "Only one can remain". On the other side, there are the ones who are exclusive and break things apart. The wave of nationalism and small-mindedness that is palpable in the old continent just at the moment of planning the Constitution of a united Europe is a good example of this. On one side the Micro, on the other extreme, the Macro, each pulling and contrasting. The same forces at another level are present in our little Martial reality and as in the previous case, the masses are brought hither and thither by the tides without even perceiving its game.

In my opinion, it is necessary to seek complements in opposites before sterile and absurd confrontation. Maintaining the identity of the styles shouldn't disallow our knowing how to enjoy the advantages of the unity of action, which are many and very positive. For that, respect is a good departure point sine qua non, but so is practicing the widening of one's view, generosity, and a little humility (and I know that that is already a lot to ask in our sector!). Nonetheless, we must be conscious that while said unity is not habitually found settling into something continuous and accepted, the leaders won't know how, won't dare, to take on actions that would undoubtedly be reflected in a much higher level of social acceptance of our practices, as well as an undeniable popularization of said practices, with all that it implies by way of advantages for the sector, in general.

From this magazine, we insist month to month with words and facts on said direction and to the extent of our capacity, we work to carry a positive message, a message of unity of action within the differences. There are still some who have not understood that that project known as *Budo International* transcends the formula of a mere publishing and audio-visual company. We haven't invented this situation: These forces, these realities, are there! There is a common determination in our collective, even for those who are not aware of it. It is about time that we all shed a little more light on the matter and that with our day to day attitude, show respect for what is different, opening our minds to other proposals without fearing the loss of our identity, and in this way we will be able to give a push as a collective toward a situation of effective unity of action and of enrichment for all.

The alternative is bad, but very bad… and with the confusion and small-mindedness, in the worst case we will wind up seeing ourselves as we are, instead of humans… fruit flies.

"The martial variety is a treasure, surely, but trying to give preponderance to the differences about that which is not common is like trying to put up doors in the countryside"

TORERO!
THE SPANISH SAMURAI

Few people know the deep relationship that exists between the Martial Arts and bullfighting. Even in Spain, contrary to what it would seem, the Art of Bullfighting is only known by a minority, known as "fans". A fan is much more than someone just interested in the subject, it is someone who lives it with passion and understands its essences, actively participating in the "party"—also known as the Art of tauromachy—from their position in the bullring. The spectators are ZEUS and his mandate unquestionable. They ascend to the altars as much as they sink into the miseries of the bullfighters, but apart from that, the crowd lives the liturgy directly, intervening, demanding, and especially feeling. The feeling of the bulls is an act of spiritual communion in the here and now. When the crowd in the bullring vibrates, it does so in unison and magically, when the Art happens, they erupt as one with the so very Spanish mantra, Olé!

Among the bullfighters, there are more and more Martial Arts practitioners. Julio Aparicio, Javier Vazquez, and of course, Rivera Ordonez, whose passion for Aikido was clear in the video in which he participated with his Masters, the Peña brothers, practitioners of the very same style as Seagal. This month we bring you a new "Master", student of Jukaikido, of Colonel Sanchis; a magnificent bullfighter of great depth and enormous humanism. Angel de la Rosa.

It is not the first text I am writing about the Art of bullfighting nor will it be the last since its wealth of nuances, its force and its profundity are reasons for continuous inspiration for every fan.

The bullfighter reminds us that we are warriors, like the bull, and that once they have launched us into the bullring of life, our destiny is to fight bravely and without hope; without escapes, without comparing, until the "supreme luck" pulls us out of this existence.

In life, as in bullfighting, the "warnings" touch us all, and whether you have done it well or poorly, what is sure is that you will not be leaving where you entered.

Bullfighting is a representation, a liturgy of the totality of the universe through its complementary opposites. Men dress like women, like dancers, in order to conquer their masculinity represented in the symbol of the ears and the tail that they hand over to the triumphant bullfighter. We test the bulls' bravery, strength, stamina, and nobility.

In the fights, softness overcomes strength, integrating both principles in a dance with lethal implications in which nothing is coincidental, nor should it be; where everything can be magic if well done; where the "truth" with capital letters certifies only a single presence, and a very tangible one! It is the presence of death. Death, the final summons, is an eternal guest at this celebration, for everyone present. For the bull, without any doubt, for the bullfighter if he loses his footing for a moment, and for the crowd, which participates in the representation, identifying outside what they carry within.

The bull symbolizes the masculine principle, black and savage death, the rigor of the straight and noble charge, ordered and ritual violence that allows us to fight them. Cows are ungovernable since their charge is not straight, but elusive, mortal, and defensive. The noble bull of the ring, on the contrary, contains itself, withdraws into itself, "humiliates" bringing the snout to the ground since in that way it will measure its competitors without necessarily having to destroy them in his battle for power in the herd.

The bullfighter is the essence of the best of the feminine, of beauty and stylization, of softness in the ways in which he dominates the noble brute from the composure of courage and the certainty of tranquility with which the female controls the center. Like this, resolutely, with sweetness, without apparent effort, gathered in their center, the good bullfighters, like females, drive men almost imperceptibly into the dance of life turning around itself.

As in Aikido, the bullfighter plays out his dance in spirals facing an unpredictable and powerful Uke. 600 kg of muscle and testosterone, ending, or beginning, according to one's point of view, in a pair of sharpened knives capable of penetrating and ripping open in seconds the best most prepared anatomy.

Its snort freezes the blood; its look immobilizes; its trotting makes the ground tremble; its speed unsettles. Only temperance, precaution, intelligence and the strictest self-control permit a bullfighter to be there and do what is necessary, bring the bull with the waving of the cape with the intelligence of the very best strategy so that it goes where it doesn't want to go, so that it goes where you order it to go.

It is the will of the bullfighter to join with the bull that allows for the miracle; but only when the bull is as it must be, noble, upright, and powerful, does the magic fill the bullring and its circle turns in an ascending spiral, raising those present in an instant of vibration and amazement, in a pagan communion that surrenders in the face of the mystery of the dance of opposites.

So it is not a coincidence that many bullfighters have felt the call of the Martial Arts in its many distinct forms. The bullfighter must forge a character that requires temperance, seriousness, depth, and grace in movement, all of them virtues that are found in a good martial artist.

Today we bring to these pages an example of what we are speaking about. Angel de la Rosa, who is a student of Grand Master Santiago Sanchis:

- "Since I started training Jukaikido, I have reinforced my ability to respond facing the bull; even my control of the distances and of the sword have improved notably," the Master tells us.

But it is concerning the sense of death where this bullfighter and I mostly amused ourselves. No, it wasn't the techniques that interested him, rather the spirit that underlies our practices that attracted him:

- "With Master Sanchis, I have learned to confront our training truthfully, with the same authenticity with which I go out into the bullring. That makes both practices something unusual for a world where everything is apparently everlasting."

And in this way, in our digressions, the same company—death—never stopped appearing.

- "Bullfighters are obsessed with death, with that of the bulls, who give us triumph or take it away, and our own, which is a continuous possibility."

Like the samurais, bullfighters have had to take a position against the inevitable, and for that the striking appearance of the shiny clothes and participating in the opening procession is in and of itself an object of respect:

- "Every time I come out in the ring, I do it with all of my being. I have prepared myself for that moment and nothing can separate me from my objective."

Our guest today is an intense bullfighter, from the old, authentic school. In that face that could have easily served as a model for those serious faces in the religious statues paraded around at Easter time one perceives the nobility and the splendor of one who lives for bullfighting, not only as a profession, but also as an attribute of the soul.

- "Bullfighting is... it is something that one can't explain with words, others better than me have tried it, but only when you place yourself in front of a real bull, red cape in hand, do you discover that you were born for this."

Master and student are also friends. Sanchis has created a group that follows the student wherever he goes to bullfight. And it is when he dresses in shiny clothes and becomes a Master that all of Sanchis's warmth becomes respect for his courage.

- "I've been under enemy fire; I've seen comrades die next to me; I've known first hand what death is, horror, but when I see how Angel enters the bullring and stands before a bull, I recognize that the serene courage that is necessary requires an incomparable manliness."

In a world of adolescents that want to live with their backs to death, the bullfighter possesses exemplary courage in the taking on of the finite, the end, as something inevitable and as a previous step to the exercising of the impeccability of their Art. What is avoidable is understanding that we have the power of choosing how to live, and how to do what corresponds to us with pride, with gallantry, with honesty, depth, and truth.

In a time without references, without positive and lasting values, the image of the bullfighter reminds us, with his example, that there is a difference, that a path does exist, a way of confronting difficulties, symbolized in the bull, and of transforming it into pure Art.

Is this not the objective of a warrior?

And for those who cry for the animal in their lovey-dovey and indulgent sentimentalism, know that if it were not for the bullfights, these noble animals wouldn't even exist; too tough for consumption, too expensive to raise and maintain in freedom as princes of the pastures. Besides, they have the privilege to be pardoned and not die in the rings; if their nobility and power are sufficiently admirable, they will receive a pardon from the crowd, something that you and I can be very sure the Tao will deny us.

Admiring these warriors, I am only left with remembering that phrase the Lakota repeated before entering battle:

"Today is a good day to die!"

THE ESSENTIAL DILEMMA: BETWEEN GOOD AND EVIL

"Hell is full of the well-intentioned!"

One of the oldest human paradigms is that which refers to the most obvious and elemental division, good and evil.

Lights and shadows battle in our mythology since time immemorial. The categorization of the world and its things is the basis of this paradigm. Without this previous work, it is impossible to establish any kind of categorization, but since man has been man, he has spent his energy in this process with such diligence that it has even led him to the creation of reason, and as a consequence, to his most widespread method, science. In its elemental form, the fundamental division was to separate the whole into two parts. Day and night, light and darkness, were without a doubt the principle references that inspired the process. Our ancestors observed that the relationship between both situations was variable; the seasons in the temperate zones established less defined cycles that those in the extreme North and South, where nights could last six months. In more southern zones, the range of possibilities unfolded in four seasons. The Moon, with its own cycles, added a very special mark to these solar variables, mitigating or increasing the strength of the Sun, referring to the full Moon and to its disappearance at the new Moon. The fundamental reference, Black and White, became a range of grays that were not that as such, rather a rainbow of wealth and variety that corresponded to the wealth of the flora and fauna of these zones.

Nonetheless, all categorization stems from placing contrasting points of reference in such a way that there is a lot or a little variety, and the wealth of our catalogue necessarily winds up establishing categories that are summed up in pairs of complementary opposites. This is the basis of all the traditional philosophies. Yin and Yang, In and Yo, Ahura and Mazda, Mars and Venus, and the Sun and Moon are some of the many, many forms that said dividing line adapted.

Really, the principles in and of themselves don't represent more than that, principles of undifferentiated forces. Yin is not better than Yang, nor the contrary. However, good and evil do in fact introduce values; this is due to the fact that they are moral categories. But, where do these visions in which a new qualitative factor appears come from?

As the categorization in pairs of opposites receives nourishment from references made from two points, man, the compulsive categorizer, discovered the possibility of establishing even more distinctions; another way of ordering the world that he perceived, establishing levels from below upward. On the horizontal categorization (rising and setting sun) he superimposed a categorization analogous to that of a mountain, where the lower part preceded and supported the upper. Each stage of this ascension implied groups of categories that had something in common. Right against left, above contrasting with below! In the end, as you see, the ancient philosophy, with all its sophistication, winds up seeming more like Sesame Street that anything else.

For the Easterners, the categorizations, like all their philosophy, fed on the image of man integrated within the grand Whole of Nature. For that, a comparison was established with the human body. The more physical matters, below; the emotions corresponding to the center; and the mental with the upper part. In the same way, they established that man could be or exist predominately more in any of these three levels, though he existed de facto in each one of them at the same time.

The moral sphere, there where good and evil exist, was for the ancients a space that ran along the line between the emotional and the mental; therefore, it wasn't considered a superior vision of the world. Above this level there was yet the intellectual level, social level, another ideological, and the most superior of all of them, that of the Sen Nin, "the men of the mountains," the level of free thought or judgment. On this plane, man didn't judge the forces as he did in the previous, rather he integrated them in the catalogue, understanding their function and necessity as part of the Whole that had no intention, of a Universal Order in which "it did nothing, but in which nothing was left undone;" something very far from the vision of the personal God that the West inherited from the Judeo-Christian tradition. However, even in these traditions, the symbols leave no doubts. In the first, the triangle that points to heaven superimposes itself on that which points to earth, giving rise to the star of David. The forces of Heaven descend to the earth and vice-a-versa. The Christian Cross symbolizes the same principle. A longer vertical line

(Yin) represents Heaven, and the transversal, a shorter line (Yang), the earth. In both cases, the union of both forces summarizes the harmonization of the totality of Being, divided into the two fundamental principles.

The moral plane of conscience is one of the most extended among humans. It must be recognized that it is very functional by way of simplifying everything to the contrasting of good and evil! Furthermore, as this part of us that participates in that level of conscience is in continuous interaction with the world and with others, we spend life continuously reinforcing ourselves. "God makes them and they group together," goes the popular saying. It is easy to understand, simple to execute, a marvelous remedy to judge the world without breaking one's head; nonetheless, paradoxically, this vision is the mother of much misery. How is that possible?

The moral is founded on the exclusion of a part of the Whole. Good is acceptable, evil must be isolated. However, today we know that everything in the Universe is interrelated in an untouchable interweaving, in an interdependence of infinite proportions. Therefore, nothing is alien to anything, and, how many times have those pursuing good produced great evil, and visa-versa?

For reflective man, for the conscious warrior, there is no easy road. He can't get around the fact that the most widespread formula of categorizing the world among humans is a failure..., a dangerous failure, which, however little it is pushed—a little this way, a little that way—winds up in fanaticism and destruction. It is an exclusive formula that regardless of how well-intentioned, sooner or later turns into its opposite.

PARIS IS BURNING!

Yes, Paris is burning and with it we all are a little. From these pages and for the most accustomed readers, there is already no doubt about my position in this regard, but as the "media noise" is so dreadful, and the global blunder so intense, it seems there is no choice but to repeat and repeat, and we'll see if in this way we wake up those whose conscious is sleeping and stop thinking that things will resolve themselves.

The systematic destruction of the "authoritarian" hasn't just arrived now, it is a process that began a long time ago, but in this new version of the fall of the Roman Empire, it hasn't ceased to be a less certain and essential component. Authority (and I know some will want to crucify me for this affirmation!) is a masculine figure. I'm sorry, it is an unquestionable reality, because it is a biological reality, not an intellectual or ideological opinion. One can't decide to be a mother no matter how much one pushes to be.... And as it is the structure that defines the function, I say, that in the final result, beyond the optional and the cultural, something influences these differences.

This perseverance in the disassociation of the biological and the cultural is the mother of a great deal of bad, but today, forcing things to such an extent, the distance has gone beyond saving, so much so that for saying hard truths to someone, they can call you all kinds of things except good. Just as I have made it quite clear in preceding writings, hanging the masculine is the order of the day. Everything that smells of authority, masculinity, manliness, etc., is susceptible to being criticized and underappreciated, when not demonized.

The functional characteristic of the masculine is the sense of territory. Males in all species are territorial (except the left-handed) and to defend our territory we have been given more physical volume and more strength. But it turns out (what a coincidence!) that the use of that strength is badly seen in nearly all cases in our current paradigm. Even the recourse to force in order to defend your own territory is so limited by the laws of the modern European states, that in some cases it is better for a person to let them rob and hit him than to defend himself. No! It isn't an exaggeration! Just take a look (if you have time and interest) at the legislation in your country. I'll bet everyone a few beers that your hairs will stand on end. But the bad thing is not to read it, rather to live it, as has happened to more than one friend.

The feminization of the global thinking, the "goody-goody" thinking, the "anti-masculine", is not feminine, but feminist. Real women also possess a sense of territory, but they realize it in the "nest". For that, in the majority of separations (and given that the collective paradigm doesn't act against them), they almost always wind up with the house.

The Islamic societies are masculine and since opposites attract, they are moving to Europe en masse. Of course, they don't integrate, nor will they (except in limited and therefore welcome exceptions). Second and third generations of British citizens put the bombs in London. In Paris, the same. Those behind March 11th in Spain, well, not them, they were from the "newly coined". Integration is a feminine value, just as territory is masculine.

The concept of European citizenship, of French citizenship, means nothing to one who places other metaphysical or transcendent values of great weight above it, except if reason mediates in the encounter, but reason, friends, that is a thing of the infidels! The barbarians of old didn't all arrive at once either, rather they infiltrated slowly. They were Romanized in the end; the inferior always feeds off the superior. But that left Europe in a long period of regression, a long Dark Age, which wasn't saved until the Renaissance. All that took place (as much as the fathers of the European constitution wouldn't like it) because there was a super-structure that shaped the entire matter: Christianity, and because the barbarians did not bring a common identity.

More as an ideology than a belief, Christianity established a national and referential supra-order. Nowadays, as for references, we have only "for the money", but in order for this to flow (capital is cowardly), it is necessary to have an order, and the social cataclysm we have got ourselves into does not offer it. Capital requires work, and the last to arrive are the ones who have to push upward. If the activity is strong and there is demand, then the thing flows as much as the permeability of the social layers allows. In America, as it is a younger and less structured society, one can ascend in the muddle; in Europe, one born into the Bourgeois has to be really bad to die a laborer... but at the same time, the last in line finds a lot of opposition to move up.

The pyramids of growth on both sides of the Mediterranean are so distant that more than statistical data, it seems one contemplates the graphic description of a physical law, that about the connected test tubes. The inequalities about per capita income, the cultural and educational distances, do not help the process at all; but it is the vision of the world on both sides of the mare Nostrum—the one masculine, the other feminine—which are in the end, and in my opinion, the overall determiners in the present clash of civilizations. With an impotent Europe incapable of ending these situations, of limiting the migratory flow, not even with reason (it is only addressed with contracts and rules), and much less by force (something masculine? No way!), can the battle be won, in the end.

The incidents at the Spanish border of Ceuta and Melilla are a good example of this. It wasn't by the dissuasive means of the Spanish government (soldiers without ammunition!) that the assaults on the border fences were detained. As is known, the Moroccan authorities shot to kill and afterward ended the ordeal picking up those who were wandering around in the desert. Unfortunately, the situation has already come to this. The only thing left for me to do is to quote Sun Tsu: "When a tiger guards the narrow pass, ten thousand deer won't pass."

In order to avoid things reaching the extremes, it is necessary to act with wisdom, with anticipation, but our world and its paradigms have us so imprisoned, our arrogance is so great, that we haven't been able to question our system of values to act in time, so now we have to advise the surgeon to extract the bad that, after taking so much "anesthesia", has left us stupid and silly, and not even the anesthesia works, so, in exchange for money, we ask others who are still "whole" to do the dirty work, but let us not know about it!

Now that Pandora's Box has been opened, let's see who the handsome one is to close it. It will be a pretty woman! And with this affirmation, I establish myself as a prophet for the first time! Because they have been taking off men's pants in this society for some time now, and we have to suffer the consequences!

As martial artists, the last and best masculine stronghold, we have an unwritten responsibility: To work on the education of those dear to us in some Arts so they don't argue about whether strength is bad, about whether we have or don't have the right to defend our territory, about what the inalienable rights are of the guy who is attacking us, about the "universal goodness of all beings", or about whether your god—oh, infidel—is a lesser god. No. Whatever your style is, our Arts stem from a biological premise: that territory exists, and its front-line is your physical being. Consequently, they teach you how to defend it. Funakoshi said that what you learn with your body you never forget. Train the Arts! Teach the young! Let's see if in this way those who come later, with the mess that we leave them, will at least have a trace of remembrance of what it means to be a man. Take care of yourselves; there are only a few of us, and getting fewer all the time.

BUDO THE ESSENCE OF ETERNAL JAPAN

When the way of the warrior appears before us through the perspective of Eternal Japan, the first thing that reaches us, that touches us, is a certain formal meaning, a kind of cult of emptiness.

The first thing that is transmitted is not the ethics of the warrior, rather it is his aesthetic that entrances us.

The sense of beauty, the Japanese aesthetic contrasts, it is on the opposite side of Western Baroque. The beauty of silence as opposed to the saturation of the senses; the Koto or a symphony orchestra; Rubens as opposed to some strokes by Shodo.

That is not a coincidence, it is the fruit of a super-populated civilization, of reduced spaces, limited by islands.

Order is not, then, a choice, it is a necessity, as is cleaning, the multi-functioning of the empty and interchangeable spaces with the folding screens that are moved, rice panels that are moved or that disappear as opposed to cement walls. It is a beauty, an aesthetic of sobriety. Only in this way have the Japanese people been able to reach their high level of life and development.

In order to understand the hidden soul that arises out of this formal vision, in those empty spaces where the light filtered through the Shoji plays with the shadows, one must understand the containment and the temperance that they allow. These are the result of a vision of the world strongly linked to their warrior heritage, to the rest of the Samurai culture, profoundly injured by Zen Buddhism.

The Middle Ages went on chronologically longer than it did in the West. The society organized in social classes and castes didn't evolve in the same way precisely because it stiffened its movement forward, mainly anchored on the existence of a warrior class. It was the fall of this that facilitated the rise of a bourgeoisie class of traders that wound up permeating the rigid class system. All that happened, however, without a revolution as happened in the West. The new and rising classes always tried to deeply penetrate and appropriate as much the aesthetics as the fabulous ethics of its admired Samurai caste, their heritage arriving to our days full of vitality and meaning. The Daimio of old are now the great corporations, and the Samurai and their legacy exist protected in a vision of life that transcends the specific occupations of the individual, becoming an inseparable part of the very national soul.

For the majority of us who live part of this culture through the martial practices developed in that tradition, Japan is a beacon, a reference that goes beyond our practice on the tatami. What is Japanese is a summary that beats with and exudes an almost spiritual martial message.

Nowadays, even in the West, the Oriental aesthetic, and especially Zen, has found a pronounced echo in many Arts. Architecture, urbanism, or interior design, even music, have all undergone powerful influences of minimalism and the Zen aesthetic; all of that to a great extent as a reaction to the hyper-saturation of the senses that provoke the modern, accelerated life and the enormous overload of information, pressure and anxiety.

The sight rests in the emptiness of a tea room or in a traditional Dojo; the ears recover in the silences interspersed with the arpeggios of the Koto; the taste buds delight in their unsweetened tea; they are stimulated by their spicy wasabi or are comforted in the warmth of their silk or in the warmth of their cotton with which their elegant kimonos wrap us.

The modern sportive formulation of the Martial Arts has forced, through its necessary emancipation from the origins on its path toward becoming Universal, a gradual loss of those cultural contents. With that, the youngest, who haven't known said relationship, live permanently divorced from the transcendent that exists in these Arts. An irreparable loss that sooner or later will lead them (once the competitive stage is over) to the inevitable distancing from their practices, and what is even more lamentable, to a Cartesian reduction of the ineffable that is in them to a functional equation to win in the framework of some pre-defined rules. What remains of the Universal in such a proposal? Once stripped of all its valuable wrapping, little or nothing differentiates that Judo from tennis.

Continent and content are One in the concept of Japanese culture. Mishima said of his home that there only the invisible was Japanese. And just as the title of that magnificent book by Michael Random reads, Japan is "the strategy of the invisible".

I find that in the end, aesthetics can act as anchorage, as an entrance to a vision of the world, a sensibility, without which the Martial Arts remain orphaned and without meaning. It is as if to eat, they served you the shell of the egg and took away the white and the yoke.

The Japanese aesthetic that invades us is a lesson and an opportunity to remember that not everything in the Martial Arts can and should be its "efficacies". In these matters of existence, one confronts daily much more by way of misfortunes than with a knife. Bewilderment and acceleration kill more today than pistols. Pressure and a sense of unease destroy more than hired assassins; anxiety and depression more than soldiers. And that is so because they kill the soul before the bodies, which inevitably accompany them afterward, leaving in the meantime a world plagued by zombies that eat, defecate, and have sex.

The Japanese beauty and aesthetic are not a luxury or formal etiquette; they are a focus, a way of seeing. As in good paintings, the eye of the observer is what finishes them; their value is in suggesting instead of explaining; to make one feel instead of reason; intuit instead of prejudge. The end result of that way is as indescribable as the harmony of a Ikebana, as the peace of a Japanese garden. This is not learned by techniques, it is not taught in a manual. It is a personal legacy of the one who has the gift and the mastery to move toward what he or she desires with the force that only the deep yearning of the Eternal gives.

The way of the warrior does not possess an ethic, but an Ethos, a personal "style", (Oh, paradox!) but Universal, which allows a man to tread the world with sobriety and strength. Who can offer the same?

RECOVERING THE NATURAL

"When the Tao is lost, there is virtue,
When virtue is lost, there is justice,
When justice is lost, there is righteousness,
When righteousness is lost, there is ceremony,
Now ceremony is the shell
Of loyalty and faith,
And the beginning of confusion."
Lao Tzu. Tao Te Ching

Martial Arts, in their highest sense, are not disciplines restricted by closed norms; they are a path of knowledge of oneself and of the All. The specific aims, the utilities and multiple specializations that you can find in them are, considering the aforementioned, something spurious and dispensable. Yet, with the passing of time, and the loss of the original meaning, they have multiplied in their forms, ways, and contents. This has produced a magnificent proliferation of disciplines, and this has permitted the appearance of experts, styles, and formulas that undoubtedly offer a magnificent range of cultural wealth. However, the greatest wealth is nothing compared to the Tao. For that, we must periodically reconsider everything together and revise our intentions to penetrate this Martial path, and who better than Lao Tzu as a companion on this voyage:

When the Tao is lost, there is virtue,
When virtue is lost, there is justice,
When justice is lost, there is righteousness,
When righteousness is lost, there is ceremony,
Now ceremony is the shell
Of loyalty and faith,
And the beginning of confusion.

The Martial Arts in their most modest but highest exposition could be a path toward the re-encounter with the very essence of ourselves. The essential is the direct relationship with our Being and with the World that lies behind duality. It is the pathway of the eternal return to our origins, the ability to realize the unity of all things without losing the awareness of our Being.

No. It isn't easy to approach this subject. Every time we try, we rub up against the inaccessible, the untouchable, and indefinable, but at the same time, it should be very simple. Take the example of one stone striking another stone. The spark is not an act posterior to the strike, rather something synchronous. However, in our mind we can draw the one as a step toward the other, like a cause leading to an effect. In this way, ordering the world, we begin to distort it, to betray its simple and straightforward truth, and this is nothing more than the spark arising at the same time the stones strike each other, not afterward. If our mind stops to consider the matter, it first has to pass through one place in order to arrive at another, and in that way we will always arrive late. In the same way, seeking in the results the virtues inherent on the Martial path is by itself a predisposition to restrict our journey toward true and complete success.

"All roads lead to Rome," goes the old adage. In that sense, we can say the same of the Martial Arts. Approaching any one of them is to take a step in that direction. What really differentiates is the attitude of the neophyte. At the beginning, everyone in one way or another finds themselves dazzled by the techniques and their results. It would be like what Bruce Lee, emulating the Taoist tradition, said about fixating on the finger that points to the moon in such a way that one confuses it with the moon itself.

The supreme objective of Martial Arts is frequently not visible to the eyes which have not penetrated deeply into this matter. Nonetheless, the driving force behind its quest is common to all beings. For that, the true Masters invariably detect it behind the anxious and hungry looks of their new students. Their true labor, more than teaching a technique, is that of not letting them go off course, not letting them lose themselves in the thousand and one twists and turns that this path holds. It needn't even be said that Masters like these are few and far between. The majority simply try to leave their stamp, transmit their version, lift their ego and their "way" to the heights of the Universal, perpetuating their errors and their skills and in that way satisfy their defects and holes, which will be many since only the Tao itself (our sense of Unity with the All, conscious, fluid, natural) can infinitely fill everything and everyone. When the Martial Arts are taken as a way to knowledge, it is a path of detachment more than a path of accumulation. The first thing that one must leave aside is arrogance. This happens at comprehending one's own awkwardness. However, when this is rectified and the black belt is around our waist, one must re-start the process, unlearning the technique in order to find naturalness. We already know how the selective pyramid of the Dojo works. Of a thousand "white" belts that begin, one achieves a "black". Another far less visible selection occurs from that point onward. In this even greater selection, from a million "black" belts, only one passes to the next stage and finds their natural movement, forgetting, letting go of, what was so difficult to amass at the onset. In the process, the worn down "black" belt once again becomes symbolically "white".

Is this a path for everyone? The numbers say no, but the Tao says yes. In the end, all beings try for that Union that comes from perfect, impeccable, natural, fluid, and simple action; economical but effective; powerful but gentle. Order tells us that nothing is better or worse. The superior is not better than the inferior, but it is undoubtedly different.

The Martial Arts as a way respond to a Universal yearning, to a silent and inescapable calling, a longing to return to the underlying, a return to the home that we never really left. It is our consciousness of Being that encages us, our mind focused on the details, our arrogance and the desire to wear "glasses" to read the world and interact with it. When one follows the Martial path without sidetracks, one winds up taking them off and discovering that they are not necessary; but that, if it comes, takes its time since total wisdom is and will always be the privilege of the old ones.

SLAVES OR WARRIORS?

"Let us raise a standard to which the wise and honest can repair;
the rest is in the hands of God".
George Washington

"As I would not be a slave, so I would not be a master".
Abraham Lincoln

The founding fathers of the United States of America arrived to the New World dreaming of freedom. For them, freedom began with the absence of persecution, in their case religious. The fathers of the American constitution went further. They believed that freedom was something more than a right of the individual, it was the means "sine qua non" for everything else to work. This wisdom and this vision were not unrelated to their learned past, to the inheritance of the Masonic tradition, whose consequences nowadays preside over North American life, even on their dollar bills, full of symbols like the compass, the pyramid, or the famous "In God we trust". The problem with freedom comes when we want to regulate its functioning in order to facilitate the adequate conditions necessary to establish said freedom, to make it work. The modern states of rights must carry the weight of this contradiction on their shoulders. The problem is that with the passing of time, the rules change with the costumes (mores). New circumstances and discoveries have to be organized and each time there are more and more things regulated and to regulate. The result of this organizing maelstrom is that freedom shrinks with inverse proportion to the growth of laws, decrees, norms, etc.... With the passing of the years, an accumulative process is necessarily produced. In consequence, freedom begins to be a "rara avis".

There are more and more of us in the world and citizens leave others to represent us, assume they are going to represent us, and yield to them. Well, up to here, fine. This is what we suppose democracy is, with all its defects, the "least bad of the government systems man has invented." Nonetheless, such an obsession to legislate everything is finishing with freedom and with common sense. Little things that are assumed natural demonstrate how far we are from being truly free. An aseptic example of that is the obligatory use of seat belts in cars. But who is the state to legislate that matter? As long as I don't hurt anyone in my action, what gives them the right to force me to use that device? Even to fine me if I don't use it! Aren't I the owner of my own body? Or is it a mere usufruct that I receive from his "magnificence" until having to return it (I hope well used) at the end of my days when I turn into crude oil or ashes that will adorn some corner of my homeland?

The bad thing about these things is that they begin with the hand… and a short time later they take your arm. You will understand that it doesn't bother me that much to wear a seat belt, but it very much bothers me that they force me to do it. Every time I get into the car, that act is a reminder that social fascism is advancing with giant steps, a reminder that that monster of a thousand arms—which, on top of that, lives off of us—is occupying more and more of my own space, and is growing and growing.

All things carry within them the germ of their own destruction, all things carry their opposite within, and with time and space, every being, every thing, turns into its opposite. Democracies are getting more fascist by the day and as a consequence, less democratic. The form is conserved in this and that, but some factors that we assume as "normal" are, in my view, the mistaken symptoms of a cycle change. Some examples:

The usurpation of public space (we have to pay just to park!); the systematic destruction of the middle classes (there are more and more with less and less); the legislation of the private, instead of being left in society's hands and to its agility in deciding (seat belts in the car; homosexual marriage, yes or no; smoking here, but not there; I can buy alcohol in this place, but not in that other, etc., etc.)

Another symptom no less important is the systematic turning of people into zombies. You only have to turn on the television to see what's being offered and if you are smart, you understand the implicit ideologies and messages in such an offer; to say nothing of the education on offer, the tendency toward technology and specialization, without humanities, without teaching one how to think! Let us be aware of what is happening.

In this framework, the "martial education" acquires greater and greater value, but it must be exercised with responsibility and with knowledge of all that is at play. A martial instructor is always something more than a standard teacher. He or she is an educator who acts that way even if unwittingly, since he or she "speaks" to the body of his students, becoming a reference, a model, one who will possibly establish guidelines throughout the life of the students. It's likely that we can't substitute the social situation that they will see themselves exposed to, but if we can return to them, through the powerful weapon of Martial teaching, some master guidelines that inoculate the germ of the passion for truth, for the noble spirit, for responsible action, for the value of effort as a good that is not separate from their own lives, nor will it ever be. We can show them by our example the differences between positive and negative; respect for what our ancestors have left us; the value of changing in the future that which must be transformed and the respect for life itself, teaching them in first person how fragile it is. We can make them see their weak points and their strong points. Give them the chance to learn that much of what they see as insurmountable limitations can and must be overcome. Teach them also to accept that which can't be overcome since that, too, is a reality and sooner or later life will demonstrate it, so it's better that they are prepared for when that happens.

In a society that sends signals that are more and more confusing about what is positive and what negative, where the systematic "anesthesia" of individuals is fomented, where freedom is a chimera moving further and further away, the Martial Arts are a cry in the desert that affirms with power that man can be something more in life than a simple and miserable slave.

Freedom is a daily conquest, not a received right; in that, as in all things, one has to deserve it.

THERMO-REGULATION
THE MOST POWERFUL "TECHNIQUE" IN THE WORLD

"Every alteration of health,
internal or external,
has its origin in our weakness."
José María Sánchez Barrios,
from the book "Polar Universe". Eyras Publishing.

"Given the privileged situation of your situation with this magazine and the many styles and Masters you have known, what in your opinion is the best of the Martial Arts?" If we substitute "the best" for "the most effective", you will get the question that people most often ask me once they find out what I do. I always have to answer by saying that all the Arts are valid and that there aren't Arts, rather artists, etc., etc...

I know they are asking me something different, but the focus of their question is something I don't share, so for that, one might say that "I don't know," which is the correct response to their question... Furthermore, I believe that no one knows. I am convinced that every person who trains in a specific style is naturally putting his or her confidence in that style simply by dedicating their time and attention. What greater act of support can one do for something or someone? It is undoubtedly an act of love that must always be respected.

One can say the same about the question concerning what the most powerful technique is. In my opinion (and in that of many other Masters that I have known), "to injure" is always much, much easier that "to heal"; for that, my reply to that question involves a healing exercise instead of one involving damage or destruction. A wise Spanish saying tells us that, "He who can deal with a lot, can deal with a little." So, I'm not ashamed in any way to dedicate a response to this question, to share with you what I consider the most powerful tool that anyone can learn to use to improve their health, their internal/external balance, and as a consequence, their warrior capacity: thermo-regulation.

Thermo-regulation is an exercise that I've been practicing every day for many years, an exercise that any person can do to stay healthy, and even improve it, as well as reaching a more alert mental state. The master who taught me (Jose Maria Sanchez Barrio) rescued it from tradition and refined it in an extraordinary manner. He re-named it and explained the reasons for its tremendous effectiveness in physical, energetic, and modern medical terms.

It is not the first time that I'm sharing this with the readers of this magazine (nor will it be the last time). I have demonstrated that despite its extraordinary effectiveness and simplicity, thermo-regulation requires persistent repetition to be assimilated, and mostly, to go from the words to the facts. This is so to such an extent that I coined a phrase (in the times of the structuring of the system) that my mentor always repeats in his classes and I suppose he will continue doing so:

"In order to become a thermo-regulator one must be initiated by another thermo-regulator". Well, given that that is not possible through this medium, I will use all my skill with a pen to try to communicate to you and transmit to you the importance and the power of this exercise.

The power of fire and water

Thermo-regulation deals with the use of the elemental forces, Fire and Water, to restore the internal/external balance of warm-blooded beings, in general, and humans, in particular. One of the most effective vehicles for applying this technique is water. The use of water has been, since times immemorial, a source of health for our species and the systems developed for its use in the different cultures are as wide and varied as the cultures themselves.

Water is the most efficient and abundant transmitting element on the planet. For the Chinese, water, "water energy", defines the starting point of the cycle of the energies and forms; something that makes sense since life itself came from water.

The nature of this force is that of "going downward", penetrating everything, not resisting, flowing. Its opposing force is Fire, whose nature is that of "going upward", illuminating and accelerating. The combination of these forces is the creator of all that exists, or said in another way, all that exists has, in different doses and qualities, unequal charges of these two elemental forces.

In Japan, the Ofuro, the hot bath, is more than an exercise in hygiene. The cold baths beneath waterfalls while the practitioners do

Mudras and recite Mantras, are images that are in no way removed from the Martial Arts. Who isn't aware of the baths in the Ganges in the Hindu tradition? I am sure that some have even heard about the yogic hydro-therapy of Ramacharaka and of the multiple exercises, or Kriyas, in which water is used in unthinkable ways for a Westerner.

The same Christian tradition is marked by water. The first faithful ones identified themselves and the places they occupied with the symbol of a fish. In fact, the Christian is a Christian from the moment in which an "initiated one" pours the "sacred water" over them. John the Baptist "initiated" Christ by giving him a good soaking. But as Lao Tzu says: "when the Tao is lost… there is ceremony". The ceremony practiced today that goes back to those times, with all its paraphernalia, can't seem very much like the original. I have the conviction that that ceremony from the Jordan was also something more than a rite. Jesus was, of course, a person of enormous power and the personalities of power practice powerful techniques and formulas, and thermo-regulation is just that. Wanting to reduce that rite to a casual or symbolic event is to underrate its participants. "The church has doctors" goes the saying, so that this subject must be studied by others who are more versed in the matter than I am (I'm happy to leave suggestions!). The Jewish people have a similar tradition, and even converts must go through a ritual stepping naked into a pool. The powerful techniques are just that because of their effectiveness when it comes to getting results. I have been practicing this technique for many years, and there is no doubt that I've been able to test it in the most varied circumstances, with excellent results. The objective of this is essentially to regulate the temperature of our organism through an exercise that stimulates said natural function.

Any and all regulation of the temperature in the body is an action considered essential for life and is automatically controlled by laws that are in essence not very complex: the temperature mustn't rise above 42° C or drop below 35° C. Thousands of mechanisms make it possible for the body to be constantly making decisions to this respect.

Our "heating" system doesn't essentially differ from what we have in our homes. The principle distributors of heat are the arteries and veins, but instead of carrying water, they carry a salty red broth with a composition very similar to that of sea water: blood.

For Easterners, body heat is controlled by a meridian that involves various organs and that is known as the thermo-regulator meridian. On this meridian, there are three key points, known as the three burners; but I don't want to lose myself in too many technical details; let's just say that "the heat of the viscera and of digestion are distributed by the heart" which in the end is the same that Western medicine says.

In order to cool the system, the body has a very efficient interchange: the skin. Besides that, the system cools down through breathing and with the elimination of liquids and solids. Every orifice is a point for the exiting of heat and the majority of them are in the head, the place where the level of heat, tension, and activity is the maximum for human beings. The nervous system and its central computing system produce some exceptional heat levels and the maintenance of the temperature in this area is critical. Furthermore, the heat, the Fire energy, tends to rise just as Water energy tends to go down, so that the head is well equipped for regulating temperature. The Chinese say: "The head cold and the feet warm".

The main mechanism for heat regulation, one that is very human, is sweat. Other mammals, such as bears or dogs, do not have this gift from nature. For that, they pant frequently when they want to refresh the system. This is no joke: some of our ancestors failed as a species precisely because they lacked an efficient ventilation system. If the system heats up, it collapses and let's see who it is running behind or in front of another animal to hunt it or to not wind up being a snack. Refreshing the system through breathing gave the little human mammal great advantages in its habitat. It wouldn't be the strongest, or the fastest, but it was definitely one that best eliminated the excess of heat from the system.

The brilliant solution from nature was to apply humidity to the skin. Humidity is analogous to cold, it intensifies it, gives it more force, but most of all, water is one of the most efficient heat transports that exists. When water, or sweat, makes contact with warm skin, it generates little rising spirals of vapor which, in the most efficient way possible, carry the heat outside the body. A few little hairs facilitate this, but many make it more difficult; this is one of the reasons for the loss of body hair in our species. Given that in our body the sources of heat are internal, the ways of being able to evacuate its excess quickly are fundamental for the good functioning of the system and for the maintenance of the balance of life, which we call health.

Seen from a basic perspective, Interior and Exterior are complementary opposites. When one pole is warm, the other is cool. In this way, when we have a fever, the thermal sensation is of cold since the temperature sensors are in the skin and this is situated on the outside.

From the perspective of Center and Periphery, things are the same. As martial artists we know very well that the center of gravity, the energetic center, and even geometric (remember Leonardo's drawing of a man with his arms open!), is in the lower abdomen, the Tan Tien, or Hara. When there is a fever, the periphery, the hands and feet, are cold. From the Above-Below perspective, the matter is no different since Fire is an ascending energy, so that when there is fever, the head heats up while the feet get cold.

Thermo-regulation as a technique utilizes the natural mechanisms of the body and comes from the elemental forces of nature, Fire and Water, to regulate temperature with methods (and what is no less important!) with natural strategies. To reach this objective, the thermo-regulators use cold water to get rid of excess heat as well as to stimulate the circulation, which is the same system that naturally does said task.

The application and its "Golden Rules"

Cold water is a powerful tool, but as with all powerful weapons, it must be used wisely in order not to provoke the opposite effect of what is being sought. If we were to let the cold penetrate to the interior, we would be doing just that, therefore, in all thermo-regulation techniques, said action must be avoided.

Given that the body must remain in a constant and limited range of temperature, the biological mandate is imperious: where it gets cold, blood is pumped to warm it up. If we do cold water applications on the skin, the body pumps blood to the periphery. The blood is cooled and when it returns to the inside, it lowers the overall temperature. It's the same thing that nature does and even the same that the body tries to do with a fever.

In order to avoid the cold from penetrating to the inside, there is a golden rule in thermo-regulation. "Never apply cold water on cold skin and never leave the skin cold after the application".

The same idea in reverse is also true: "Never apply warm water on warm skin, nor leave the skin warm after the application". So, many of you are not doing yourselves much of a favor by showering in hot water just after coming out of training when you are all warmed up!

Hippocrates, the great father of medicine (so misunderstood these days by the virus hunters who endanger his principles), put it very clearly: "Nature is what heals". His two other essential principles were: "Don't damage," and afterward, "clean". Thermo-regulation abides by all these principles

always when the Golden Rule is applied: it doesn't damage; later, it cleans (inside and out!); and finally, it acts by stimulating and utilizing the same processes that nature has given us to maintain life.

The correct use of warm and cold water should be a first-year course for all human beings; however, its is a subject that we have deferred to the simple criteria of "likes" and given that the likes of our time are "soft and softening", the abuse of warm water is a constant around the world. This is so even among many martial artists, capable of extreme effort and acts of will in their training, but incapable of simply taking a cold shower after finishing their classes. Such is the weakness and lack of criteria which I find myself dealing with at proposing this system. For that, I have seen that the initiation, as John did with Jesus, is in this question an almost unavoidable act, except when I discover, joyfully, that there are still some brave individuals, some warriors, with sufficient courage to take advantage of this powerful technique, daring to try it.

There is a lot that could be explained about this technique, about its advantages and about the many positive effects it produces, and why. And one day I will do so in greater detail. Meanwhile, I challenge you to feel its effects on your own flesh and in first person. Just remember that it is essential to warm up before apply cold water. A kata? A fight? A race? And afterward, you already know: Cold shower! Then quickly dry yourself and cover the skin with appropriate clothing. Repeat as much as you like, but do me the favor of giving yourself at least three… Don't be prudish!

If, when you leave the gym after this exercise, your skin doesn't glow and your eyes don't sparkle, if you don't perceive smells with greater intensity like you did when you were children; if you don't notice your body relaxed, but firm and active; if you don't feel awake, alive, and happy, it's simply because you did it very wrong indeed, or that the accumulated "thermal contamination" is tremendous!

There is no technique that I know of as powerful for strengthening the body and the spirit of a warrior; there is no more intense Chi Kung, nor more powerful Kata, nor any hidden technique that can give you more satisfaction or power that that of surrendering yourself to the natural and intense pleasure of feeling the intense massage of the elemental forces that thermo-regulation offers you.

"Thermo-regulation as a technique utilizes the natural mechanisms of the body and comes from the elemental forces of nature, Fire and Water, to regulate temperature with methods (and what is no less important!) with natural strategies"

SOCIETY, COMMUNICATION, STYLES, AND MARTIAL ARTS

"The wise man doesn't say everything he knows,
but thinks everything that he says."
Artistoles

There are many friends who are kind enough to read this editorial page. There haven't been a few occasions in which they have asked me to increase the typography of my text.

Notice that, in their kindness, they didn't say: "Alfredo, you write too much!" Rather: "Why don't you add a page to your editorial and that way we can read you better... Your editorials are already dense enough for forcing the brain without having to force the eyes as well."

Sympathizing with them (I, too, have to use glasses to read), I have at last taken the step of carrying out their desires. I take advantage of the situation to thank all those who read these pages, and the friends who make comments through e-mails, or in the meetings here and there around the world on my trips. Thank you for your support and sympathy.

After seventeen years editing this magazine in various languages, one of our original desires is having wonderful results: An international community of scholars and lovers of the Martial Arts who maintain a common meeting point, a collective reference, who vibrate together, sharing knowledge, novelties, information, and interest, through this living and changing vehicle that is our magazine, *Budo International.*

This is a fact without precedent as far as the disciplinary Arts are concerned, and in my opinion, it marks a milestone in the globalization of all that makes up our world of common interests.

Magazines and their influence in recent Martial history

In the seventies and eighties of the past century, the American revolution was seen with the advent of personalities who, questioning the Eastern tradition, and focused on the desire to approach realism more and more, developed syncretic Arts and systems.

It was the Golden Age of the magazines in the U.S., Bruce Lee, Chuck Norris, Ed Parker, Ninjitsu, Full Contact... the sales were fabulous! The Martial Arts inundated everything! In Europe, some fortunate ones read these magazines and were up to date. Bushido in France established the guideline, and though it was only published in France, it was the European reference in the sector. Other magazines, always in an exclusively national context, informed us of a world of novelties and Masters, always two steps behind that guideline established by the North American revolution.

When we published the number 1 edition of *Budo International* in the Spanish language, we felt something big was about to happen. It didn't take long for us to understand the universal vocation of our project, and not without a lot of effort, and no less errors, we put the first versions in other languages on the market. The Portuguese edition was the first; then came the French edition. The edition in the Italian language was our next step, followed by *"Kampfkunst"* (Arts of Combat), which is how we called the German edition. This was followed by the edition for Great Britain, *"Black Belt UK"*, and finally the edition for the United States of America and Canada, *"Budo International America"*. Some friends from other magazines already being published in countries like Czechoslovakia or Greece, joined ours, including a great deal of our articles as the backbone of their editions, and of course, not to forget that untiring adventurer, our friend Zoran Rebac, who immediately after the conflict in the Balkans, took the chance with a Croatian edition, an area where *Budo International* is the leader and reference.

During those years, we led many changes in the sector. We were the first magazine in Europe to interview a Gracie and have him on the cover, giving him the due importance that they later had in our world. The Vale-Tudo revolution found us on the front lines when nobody even knew what it was. We were the first in adequately valuing the importance that the field of security and reality-based Martial Arts were going to have in our sector when nobody, absolutely nobody, bet on it. We have saved Kyusho Jitsu from ostracism and revealed some of the biggest values of our times, being informed and discovering ancient and ethnic Martial Arts that were virtually unknown, and we have established an unquestionable reference among professionals from all over the planet.

Out of all of that, what most pleases me is having been able to establish a higher standard in terms of quality in our sector.

The magazines have improved a lot in these years; our pressure on the publishing sphere so that it would improve the presentation of its products has not been in vain. Our magazine never stopped adding pages, more color, better quality paper and binding, as well as more respect for the client, for the reader, offering better written texts, not interrupting here and there to send them to page 191, etc., offering a variety of contents, the inclusion of novelties, and audio-visual references with quality videos, etc.

The Martial "businesses"

The Martial world has changed and we haven't ceased doing so as well; however, the companies in this sector have not accompanied this growth. They continue wedged into their reference markets, and save some laudable exceptions in Europe (*JUTE Sport* in Italy with the purchase of *Sportimex* in Germany, *FUJI Mae* in Spain, especially with its expansion in France and Belgium), the majority haven't jumped the borders of their sphere of influence more than anecdotally or temporarily.

The big franchising companies of the sector like Adidas are gaining ground here and there, but they have had to get over bad times and restructuring that have slowed their speed of growth and implantation. It's sure that a much less uncertain future is opening up for that company with the appearance this past year of new projects, seemingly having decided to take the necessary measures for things to work. Other renowned brand names continue ignoring the Martial Arts.

America in crisis?

It's good for everyone that the sector is strong and successful. The best things appear when these circumstances arise, as much for the users as for the companies. However, there are still critical points that we can't neglect to analyze. The distribution of magazines in America is not a difficult task these days and magazines with a long trajectory, true icons of the American market, sell in almost laughable quantities if compared to the vitality of the European market. As evidence of that, the sector adapts and re-adjusts, suffering since our appearance in America continuous transformation, where the ownership of the old famous magazines changes hands continuously. Even I was offered the chance the buy one of them at one point! There is a very patent separation between sectors in America and an atomization of them in an old market that is powerful for its size and unity. Some believe that the answer is in more "grappling", or in more "specialization", but they are wrong; the answer is in "more unity" and more "quality", at least that's how we see it in a medium and long term bet through our *Budo International* edition for America.

The disciplines

Until a few years ago, Martial Arts were a synonym of Judo, Karate, and Taekwondo. The Chinese Arts took longer to arrive and the first that many of us knew about them came through the Kung Fu series. However, in the past decades, the appearance and development of other styles, as much traditional as innovative, has given a strong push to the sector, augmenting the competition and introducing at every step new proposals so that the lay people became more and more interested in the material. From the angle of Tai Chi, Chi Kung, and other internal Martial forms, they have seduced groups of Martial practitioners in numbers that were unthinkable until only a short time ago, such as the retirement age sector. From the opposite angle, the MMA and realistic fighting, Vale Tudo, has summoned and pushed an incipient professionalization in groups of fighters. The show sector has not ceased to grow and Kick Boxing is still seeking a reference framework beyond K-1 in order to "find itself" and give of itself what it still can and must give. However, this sector finds in Europe little receptivity in the media, which still wonders whether Boxing is a sport or an activity proper of savages, something unthinkable in the USA where Boxing has always gone along freely, constituting a multi-million dollar business. Only Great Britain in Europe maintains such a tradition, what is facilitating de facto the implantation of these new varieties of combat shows. Holland also keeps its tradition very much alive in this respect, being the cradle in the West of quality Thai Boxing and Kick Boxing. For that, it has been in this zone where the new proposals have been most easily understood and accepted. The rest of Europe maintains a moral censorship, many times not explicit, but which means a definite "boot on the throat" in the new forms of combat shows. Italy seems to be one of the few nations more open to the matter, especially in reference to Kick Boxing.

Nonetheless, the great granary of the Martial Arts continues being its practice as Martial Arts or combat sports. I analysed this at length in a previous editorial, comparing both sides of the coin, the two opposing models, France and the United States, state intervention against organizational liberalism. Europe is living a specialization like it has never seen in this sector. The national teams of the main world powers of Karate, Judo, and Taekwondo possess exclusive dedication, specialized trainers, high quality installations, international leagues, etc. The pool of athletes continues training as always in their gymnasiums, and many times there is no connection at all with competition. Groups formed around a particular Master are not rare, or followers of this or that style, with insurmountable differences in terms of technique, kata, or forms. Judo continues being, "Judo", one and monolithic, introduced less and less in the gymnasiums in the street, and more in schools, and with an elite of magnificent, high-level competition in countries like France and Great Britain. Taekwondo has overcome the division that came from the death of its founder, and at least in Europe, has clearly imposed the Poomes and the WTF system. In America, Taekwondo continues as it was in Europe some years ago, alive in regards to Masters with a unique discourse in their teaching and basing their success on leadership, and some on their worldwide fame, as is the case with John Ree. Nonetheless, Taekwondo, perhaps for the very significant Korean immigration to the USA, has its own extremely important tone and force in North America. Europe doesn't have such a clear homogeneity despite having it in terms of organizations, and that is due to the fact that not all the national Federations have been emancipated from the influence of the Korean pioneers in order to fly with their own wings. This is not about "racism", but about ways. The old ways were much more arbitrary and they worked when the groups were small and the leadership great. However, as the caterpillar in its metamorphosis, these forms as they were must die in order to reach a new state capable of "flying". Spain is a magnificent example of this success and its new and very capable president promises to undertake a great modernization, essential for giving the jump that this Art and Martial sport deserves, which would place it in a position to grow and have more influence in the Martial panorama, in general.

The small and medium size organizations are growing. Many times they offer specialized attention and work, much more personalized, and they know how to seduce clients. Some have even been marking milestones in the past decades contributing an energy and vigor that was unknown in the sector before. Once can't neglect to give an example of Wing Tsun and of its great architect, Keith Kernspecht, whose most well-known student, Sifu Victor Gutierrez, has broken molds regarding the speed and intensity of implementation of a style in more than one country. Despite some organizational differences in the heart of the EWTO, they have been the ones who have dominated the sector in Europe, students of the "Kaiser" Kernspecht, to whom no one can ever deny his vision and insight at achieving the establishment of a Chinese style in the West with such success.

Styles based on self-defense have sprouted up in the post-September 11th framework and in the tense social environment at the beginning of the century. Some of a new mold and others with long tradition are bringing innovative formulations and concepts presented by men of great knowledge and recognized ability. An example of that are the "Reality-based Martial Arts" of Jim Wagner, Krav Maga and the family of Israeli Martial Arts formulations, a country in permanent conflict that has given rise to some experts and warriors of great worth, such as Avi Nardia or Moni Aizik.

Kajukenbo, Kenpo, and other combat arts focused on real contact continue attracting new students under personal leadership rather than under the signs of big organizations, establishing novel guidelines.

Classic styles like Jiu-Jitsu are living a renaissance unthinkable even a few years ago by way of the Gracie revolution; however, they still haven't managed to seduce big sectors of the population, many of them as fascinated by as they are reluctant about the necessary identification that was at first established between Vale Tudo and Jiu-Jitsu, something that is changing little by little thanks to the untiring work of people like Grand Master Mansur or the Machado brothers, more and more focused on Jiu-Jitsu as a Martial Art and sport than as a form of extreme combat. Other big names in the sector in Europe have opened students' eyes to other Jiu-Jitsu no less

forgotten and of great interest, such as Grand Master Surace in France or Bryan Cheek in Great Britain.

Obviously, all that there are, are not mentioned here, but certainly all who are mentioned are important in this hurried summary and analysis of the Martial Arts evolution. Our place as communicators is and has been that of connecting the living forces of the sector, but also that of presenting and representing the sector itself to the rest of society. So, we are also and in some ways a "shop window" for others in the sector, and for the "non-practitioners" of Martial Arts. We do not take this responsibility lightly, being able to contribute a certain level by way of the presentation of our sector to the benefit of all of us—practitioners, companies, publishing houses, organizations, an entire world around a practice that continues and will continue changing people positively: The Martial Arts.

Thank you for your support and for allowing us to continuing doing our job; your votes are read loud and clear every month with the results of the sales of the magazine. Thanks.

GENERAL ANESTHESIA

"To fall is allowed, to stand up is mandatory."
Russian proverb.

It seems that this is the prescription given the nature of these tumultuous, apocalyptic times of Kali Yuga. The generalized daze has a multitude of variations, adopting the most varied strategies, but it is undoubtedly there wherever one cares to look.

It seems that everything everywhere has come to an agreement so that a kind of Unitarian, compassionate action, a kind of mental and physical euthanasia, is affecting human beings as a whole. Of course, far from being a matter that comes to us from the outside, we seem to be well disposed and have the perseverance to collaborate with it.

Let's look at some examples: the consumption of psycho-pharmaceuticals in modern societies has multiplied, accompanying a process of an increase in mental illness. Even a high percentage of those who are above the essential minimum and who are not categorized as socially dangerous, or "medicated", maintain a more than doubtful base when it comes to being considered mentally healthy. Some are hooked on Valium and its variations, others on sleeping pills, the case is that of being disconnected from a reality that doesn't fit, direct, or process adequately.

Illnesses of a new breed such as altruism or Parkinson's, Alzheimer, or Mad Cow, directly attack the central computer, structurally incapacitating individuals. All of that in a context that involves the same characteristics: disconnection and the inability to interact with a medium qualified as hostile. But, is nature more hostile now than before, or is it that we are weaker?

There is no doubt that the earth is immersed as a whole in a process of warming and that implies acceleration. Time tends to be squashed together and in consequence everything accelerates more and more. There is a generalized sensation of pressure; time is a rarity and more so day by day. Nowadays, in only one day we process a great deal more information than our great-grandparents did in a whole year back in their time. This "warming up" of the "meninx" is in part responsible for this situation, but it is no less the lack of fortitude that we humans show, each day more dependent on our perks, many of them the daughters of comfort, a master much crueler than we could ever have imagined.

This disposition has its results in the new and prevailing ideologies, all of them soft, sentimental, and compassionate, but only as a reflection of the very sensation of being victims, or what is the same, prey. Humans have been magnificent predators, but it seems as if we have run out of gasoline...

I'm not saying that these constants can be annulled, nor am I so optimistic as to think that the situation can be reversed. I'm only directing myself to those individuals with sufficient energy and determination to apply the adequate recipes to their lives, and in an effort to adapt, live them more truly, as well as making them a positive and luminous reference for others. On the personal level, one can oppose this state of affairs, but it requires a constant effort of awareness and work.

In the community of martial artists, there are constants that are indispensable in order to accomplish this task, since the very practice of disciplinary Arts implies a distinct perception of the world, beyond the soft and miserable discourses of the prevailing ideologies that have already affected their minds. In the end, what counts is that there is a concentrated effort, and that this takes place in a space of confrontation and not one of comfort.

It is the very practice of war that makes the warrior, what stipulates his disposition, and however much the follower has still not woken up from the generalized "dream" of living in a world of Bambis, at least their "bodies" are no longer unfamiliar with the implicit truths in martial learning. The very fact of considering the possibility of fighting instead of being prey offers a distinct vision, a perspective that is, of course, that of a NON-VICTIM.

The change could seem small, but it is substantial and its consequences can be truly profound when the student is capable of extracting all the consequences of it and extrapolating them to other aspects of his or her existence. By positioning oneself as a "non-victim", one is, for the first time, taking responsibility for one's destiny. If this direction consolidates, the change of attitude is a natural and powerful consequence. By taking responsibility, you cease to blame others; by feeling strong, you don't have to attack; from a position of power, judging others is no longer so simple, and once one has been through the experience, common in any martial learning process, of pain and defeat, one questions a great deal the methods and ways of co-habiting with one's fellow man.

The capacity to commit in order to reach black belt in any style requires a long-term determination and unequaled effort. Taking responsibility implies that phrases that include "It's just that..." or that begin with "but" are little by little removed from one's vocabulary.

The commitments are day by day less frequent among humans and the capacity to throw oneself into them a rarity. Everything is fleeting, passing, and changing like a weather vane in the wind. Everything is fashion, everything conditional. Hedonism, in this context, ceases being a virtue to become the prison of the unsuspecting and a lashing for the distracted.

It helps for absolutely nothing the idea, absolutely installed in our minds by an infinity of mediums, that we are basically immortal. At least we deny death, we put it in a corner in our societies, as with old people, who we know call euphemistically "third age". One must live in eternal adolescence, in a forced youth, and in many of their iniquitous values. And science is at the service of all of this with cosmetic surgery, hair dye, and other pathetic demonstrations of the inability to assimilate the inherent beauty of the signs of an intense life, one well lived, the signs that are left on our faces and bodies.

By not being conscious of the finite, we put off the changes and even combat them fiercely, changes that we should consciously support in order to live a life replete with personal growth and moments of plentitude, a life that cannot detach itself from the change within itself, a change that is always presented through cycles, generally well differentiated, and where each one must be lived with its own dispositions and encouragement.

The array of packaged "happiness" offered, always the fruit of the consumption of goods, generates constant alienation since they can never manage to satisfy all the caprices, no matter what one gains, no matter how much one possesses. Even being able to "buy it all", one doesn't have the time to enjoy it. This is undoubtedly a rat race, and the bad thing about rat races is that even if you win... you're still a rat. Happiness, my grandfather said, is knowing how to be satisfied. How far his words are today from the global thinking in human beings!

With this state of affairs, the only possibility for the conscious Warrior is to be constantly at war and in a state of attention in order to avoid being destroyed by stepping on one of the thousands of mines that are hidden on the road. Training, and its counterpart, deep reflection, are the weapons with which we can confront this state of things. However, we mustn't forget that everything is the product of the medium where it develops, and the surrounding medium these days is what it is.

Instead of yielding to the situation, it is in our hands to truly fight the lies, the tricks, and the hooks of juicy bait that we find here and there. The Dojo, literally "the place of awakening", is a place allied with such work. By changing our clothes, we disconnect from the day to day in order to enter into a sacred space. The debunking or the demystification of this leaves no place for the magical aspects of our psyche to be projected. Reason tyrannically imposes itself as the only "true" way, but what is certain is that it was only a short time ago when such a universally adopted truth required every corner of the human mind. We need a divine space of realization, a magic space, a point where the threshold of the daily is transcended, where it becomes the anteroom of the sacred, the mysterious, the intangible, where anything can happen. In Zen, it is emptiness, for the religious, God; in any of its forms, man needs to inhabit that space of his "self" since that makes up his primordial nature. Not leaving room for, or giving direction to this quadrant of the human soul, of the whole being, winds up arousing the flames of insanity since the ineffable invades the day to day, causing disturbances. "To God what is of God, to Caesar what is of Caesar." This co-habitation between the planes of Being that Jesus Christ proposed acquires in this sense of things a different and very pragmatic meaning. It is the animus and the anima of Jung, the unknown and the impossible to know of Castaneda, the threshold of quantum physics in the mystery of modern science.

The space of the sacred in the Martial is not, then, an empty ritual, nor something that one must disregard for being old-fashioned. Such an assumption is very proper of a society with adolescent values, where all that is modern is good and the traditional bad, by definition.

With this stupid attitude come the greatest outrages, equaled only by those of fanaticism, another of the constants in humanity's mental illness. Facing the dilemma of the mysterious, the fanatic clings to his "beliefs" in order to confront the mystery of life and death, to the point where he is willing to die or to kill for them; such is his fear. This is tremendous nonsense and an absolute inversion of terms since these things were made to serve man and not the contrary. The fanatic (from the Latin "fanum" meaning "temple") encloses his truth between four walls and repeats it in eternal litany with the hope that by the force of repetition, it will be truer. No, this is not the way of the conscious warrior, who instead of trying to impose his truth on others, attends to finding the truth within himself.

Fanaticism is the son of fear. A fear that makes him run backwards, become entrenched in his little world, adoring his golden calves. For a warrior, fear is his gasoline, untiring on his road toward the truth; a stimulating challenge, a bit of spice that encourages him not to rest on his laurels, what keeps him awake while the enemy lies in waiting. Don Juan kept his follower Carlos Castaneda alert with phases like, "If you turn quickly to the left, you'll be able to see your own death," or "Death is a warrior's best advisor." But given that we have encapsulated death apart from our day-to-day living, its role as an advisor is more difficult. Convinced that if we don't think about it, it won't come, we negate the evidence and with it we lose the only positive thing that it can offer us, continuous pressure, the pressure to live vigorously here and now, as the poet said: "With the intensity of a dying man and with the coolness of an immortal."

The martial artist must confront his fear in many of its forms. Fear of pain, looking ridiculous, defeat, his own inability, etc. And he does it in an effective way, with his body, his emotions, and with his mind, confronting it in his practice. The very fact that the Martial Arts are a practical matter, in the end, avoids it being derived from and lost in mere metaphysical speculation. In the end, there is always an attack technique to confront, a dodge that is done, something tangible. This way of bringing the material, the physical plane, to the questions confers on the Martial Arts an enormous advantage over other transcendent practices: the solidity of the verifiable is a great help when facing mystery since that is what lies in waiting behind each and every thing; paraphrasing Teresa de Jesus, "God also walks between saucepans." A slap is a slap, however you want to look at it, and in regards to the martial, that is where things begin: they go from below upward and not from above downward, as in a good bull fight, "from less to more."

On this voyage, then, the anesthesia is contraindicated; though the slaps don't hurt in the moment, they will hurt you later.

One can't remain under anesthesia permanently; one can't encapsulate oneself in a happy little world, since in the end what attracts is opposites, hardship, and in the best of cases, awakening from a hangover in a profound state of confusion. The way of the warrior involves tuning one's consciousness in order to be able to react to aggressions, to traps, and to the poisoned bait that surrounds him, to walk through life with the certainty of death, and toward the horizon of knowledge.

The general anesthesia is all around, so be attentive and save yourselves if you can!

**"For a warrior,
fear is his gasoline, untiring on
his road toward the truth;
a stimulating challenge,
a bit of spice that encourages
him not to rest on his laurels,
what keeps him awake while
the enemy lies in waiting"**

FEAR

"Only the one who has nothing to defend cannot be defeated."
Sun Tzu

If there exists a matter that is eternally present on the path of the warrior, it is fear. Fear can be the most powerful alley of the warrior. When it finds its right place, fear prevents disasters, advises the unwary, evades dangers, preserves life. However, left by itself, as occurs with all power, fear tends to become saturated with itself to the limit. Fear then turns into a danger in and of itself, capable of inhibiting the one who it inflicts, blocking all positive reactions.

Reacting against fear can itself become a danger. Some people overreact under pressure, responding in a way that is out of proportion to the situation. This is especially dangerous when the one suffering this circumstance is a security agent, since they are obliged to respond to danger in accord with the law and in a "proportional" way. Disproportional reactions of panic can provoke physical injury. The rigidity that accompanies these processes becomes a state of high tension that can lead to completely blocking the one affected, and it is even capable of producing fibril tears, dislocations, and even alternations in the balance of the bone structure resulting from the tension.

The response, the Warrior's only weapon against fear, is not its suppression, but courage. Fear is a natural emotion, it is an indispensable part of the defensive system that nature has endowed us with, and it cannot be, nor should it be, suppressed. Fear is not, then, the enemy, rather the lack of control that it provokes if it is not handled properly.

In all initiating processes, and of course in the Martial Arts, fear is a continuous object of personal effort for the follower. Fear of pain, of defeat; fear of aggression, of impotence; stage fright facing an exam; fear of injuring oneself, etc., all of them form a part of the many forms of expression that fear has and which we can find in the practice of the disciplinary Arts. Some are "physical" fears, others psychological, like embarrassment in all its many manifestations. One of them is the feeling of awkwardness that takes place in the first phases of the initiation and about which professor Paniagua wrote so clearly in his book "Martial Arts: The Mind-Body Balance". The student tries to repeat the movements, copying what he observes, but recognizes that he is incapable of coordinating himself. The image reflected in the mirror comes back as an impotent reality that does not please him at all. The most diverse Martial traditions confront this question through experience, placing the follower before his limits in order to help him overcome them. Fear doesn't disappear, but it is tempered, even acquiring a daily dimension that takes away from its greatest power given that there is no greater fear than the fear of the unknown.

In order to achieve an effective learning system, nature combined two opposite forces in us: curiosity and fear, the terror of the unknown. The value attributed to humans as a whole is more often than not mixed with our innate curiosity to experience everything, a restlessness that many ancestors undoubtedly paid for with their lives and that we see repeated frequently in our children, to the horror of parents and educators. Nonetheless, audacity is not the remedy of fear, rather its counterpart. With that I want to say that counter-posing courage with fear is not always the best alternative. Nothing, absolutely nothing, could substitute temperance to attain control over it.

Given that the greatest of the aspects of fear is ignorance, we can say that that is analogous to darkness. The greater part of fears disappear when a light is turned on and illuminates that space where personal monsters live, all of them always superior to any possible reality. Knowledge united with experience, there is the infallible recipe for developing the vaccine against fear! But we cannot always prevent the situations where our dark alley can appear. The situations in which panic can try to take over our being are infinite and no one can vaccinate themselves against all of them. For that, the warriors from all different times confronted the question under the same paradigm: The one who places himself in the worst situations will never lose the initiative. In this way, training acquires a new dimension, that of internalizing the exercise itself by way of confronting panic instead of making some concrete manifestation of fear the object of learning. Familiarizing themselves with fear and its consequences, the followers are placed on a path of understanding the mechanisms that make up the syndrome known as "fear". A syndrome is no other than a union of symptoms and a warrior confronts them with the tactical principle of "divide and you will conquer". When we cannot confront a superior enemy, we yield, but if our forces are equal to it, we can go to battle. Given that the battlefield in the matter of fear is oneself, the balance of powers is going to depend on how we use our forces. There are specific actions that encourage the enemy; each action that strengthens him to the same extent weakens us; but the inverse of that principle is equally true, so that the performance of the mind is particularly decisive in this battle.

Courage is by itself an act of power that slows the functions down, while fear always provokes an acceleration of them (panting, increased heart-rate, tension in the diaphragm, rising of the center of gravity, warming of the head, etc....). For that, the tempered warrior systematically detains the first attack undermining his breathing rate, and he does so by putting the accent on the expulsion of air rather than on taking it in, without forgetting to attend to the control of that unstoppable impulse to contract that invariably accompanies the boost of adrenaline.

Fear and Water energy

In Eastern philosophy, fear is the perverse emotion of "water" energy. For that, it has always been said that fear resides in the water entrails and organs of the body, that is, in the kidney and the bladder. Obviously, when we say kidney or bladder in the context of Eastern medicine, we are not only referring to the organ that those names refer to in Western anatomical physiology, rather to what includes other organic parts such as the adrenaline glands, whose functions possess an intrinsic relationship, perfectly described in Western medicine, with the symptoms and physiological reactions to fear. The analogous color proper of Water energy is black and obviously its elemental state is related to cold and humidity. It is curious how even in the West, all of that is perfectly familiar in our particular mythology. A typical fright scene in a movie is produced at night, in a humid environment, often with fog, preferably cold, and of course dark. There lies the perfect habitat for ghosts, monsters, and the living dead! At the same time, water energy governs the bones, and every self-respecting horror movie must have a skeleton.

The bladder and kidney meridians spend a great part of their movement moving down the back (bladder) and upward (kidney) in the back part of the legs, beginning in the large toe (interior). The legs, locomotion, and all the lower parts of the body are governed by Water energy, something that shouldn't surprise us since the natural direction of water is to go down and inward. When water rises, it does so perfidiously and the presence of such movement indicates corporal dysfunction. For example, when there is retention of liquids, they tend to rise and expand the leg tissues, first, and then flood all the rest afterwards. At the same time, for the correct function of water to be produced, and therefore for the positive functioning of fear to take place, ascendance must be avoided. The expression "I froze" frequently describes a situation of panic. The lower train must be activated positively and avoid blockage. A perfect example of that can be found in the art of bullfighting. In bullfighting, calm is undoubtedly an achievement, but the bullfighter must exude a profound relaxation in order to detach himself from a natural weakening sensation in the movements of the feet. In fact, the bullfighter, in the confrontation with the bull, must move his rear leg forward, an essential act for this depth of courage to take place and what is called, "cargar la suerte" ("to mount luck") Curiously, fear, if it is present, not only blocks the action of the legs and makes them rigid, shaky, and weak, but if it favors any movement, it is of course, the opposite, taking a step back.

The positive movement of Water energy is fluidity. In order to confront fear, then, one must act contrary to what one desires, recognizing and neutralizing its symptoms, countering the deficiencies that it provokes. Since the complementary opposite of Water energy is Fire, it is never a bad idea to add a little "positive fire" to our strategy. Enthusiasm, knowledge, light, joy, and laughter, a lot of laughter... all of them are positive fire energy, and are magnificent antidotes to fear. There is in the Shinto tradition an exercise for "distancing ghosts". The exercise in question consists of striking the palms hard on the forehead at the same time that we repeat, HA!

Death, the paradigm of fear

The paradigm of fear is undoubtedly the fear of death. Death is the door to the unknown and as we have seen, that which is hidden behind the veil of darkness and the unknown is the territory proper of fear. For that, death is undoubtedly the main ingredient of the warrior's path in any of its versions, the black death represented by the horns in the bullfights of the "Taurus-magic", the cold cut of the Samurai' katana. The very kingdom of Hades, surrounded by water, was reached in Kharon's boat.

Death was and has been the central matter in the Way of the Warrior, both symbolic death and real death. Allegorical death represented at the end of a stage, the black belt as the conquering of darkness, as an affirmation that they will never take your hara, as a symbol that you have conquered a piece of darkness on your path toward the light, the light in which time will convert your belt again, to white.

For the Samurai, the way to confront death was to incorporate it. "No one can kill the one who is already dead." The Samurai gave over their lives devotedly to the service of their master, their lives no longer belonged to them, and to such an extent that their masters could at any time reclaim it, ordering them to execute seppuku, ritual suicide, better known in the West as Hara Kiri (cutting the hara). Its tactic was drastic and was no other than putting oneself beyond the reach of fear, completely withdrawing its greatest power, the fear of death. Such an act of power didn't totally guarantee the freeing oneself of all fear since other fears could make the Samurai uncomfortable, such as the fear of failure, of not appropriately carrying out orders, fear of dishonor, etc…

As Sun Tzu says, only those who have nothing to defend cannot be defeated, and given that life, as the Bible describes, is in itself "vanity", fear's ultimate support is the very ego, personal importance. In the way of the warrior of Carlos Castaneda, fear is the constant in his training. Death becomes the advisor, and fluidity, indifference (positive water) are essential achievements.

In these current times of excess of Fire energy, one of the consequences is the lack of Water. People's kidneys must be made of phosphate since fear plays freely nearby, enslaving millions of people to that which promises some security. The insurance people are not the least of those who benefit from this situation, but we mustn't forget all the other power groups that live from it. Wrapped in their white robes and invested with the same attributes with which the Queen of England bestowed upon James Bond, the priests of medical science offer great remedies to keep death away. Meanwhile, the death that has been kept away from our daily lives—as if with that we could avert it—becomes an uncomfortable presence, a troublesome guest at the table of the new gods, men. They devote themselves to the frivolous promises of eternal youth, of infinite adolescence by the scalpel or liposuction, taking away people's excesses; the negation of aging, always considered by humans a source of wisdom and respect, is today something bothersome to hide away in retirement homes where, without the necessary stimuli, isolated from the world, the old ones degenerate toward the vegetable.

When the value of death as something that gives meaning to life is taking away from the here and now and no longer an impulse to live with decision and intensity in every moment, it diminishes its virtue, reducing it to a simple terror of emptiness, of non-being, converting it into the undesirable and terrible guest at the banquet of the living. The warrior's path passes through the integration of death and life by way of the adequate use of fear as the most powerful weapon on the road to knowledge.

"The warrior's path passes through the integration of death and life by way of the adequate use of fear as the most powerful weapon on the road to knowledge"

THE FIVE HIDDEN KEY POINTS THAT WILL IMPROVE YOUR TECHNIQUE

Are there magic formulas that improve one's learning in the Martial Arts?

From the beginning of time, man he has dedicated his efforts to looking for shortcuts that make his path toward his prey or his goals faster and more effective. If by magic formulas we understand those which automatically and effortlessly make one improve, the answer is, of course, no. As the refrain says, "There are no shortcuts without work," and this is a universal truth. But if by magic we understand that which allows us to jump forward, to advance up the hillsides shortening the way to the summit, the answer is yes, of course.

However, each evolutionary step has had a price attached to it. When you choose something, there is always a lot that you leave behind and to the side. But this is the adventure in living, the aim of the human being.

Many Masters point out that the joy is along the path, not at the end of it. Yet, one can enjoy the pleasure of the alternative routes along the path, and of course, the summit is always the summit, though this holds very diverse meanings for those who reach it. Let me explain: for some, the summit can be to reach invincibility, for other people to be able to defeat others (which isn't the same thing!), and for fewer people, to go beyond combat itself, go beyond duality.

In this context, technique is an indispensable tool for all students. It is in and of itself a shortcut in order to reach excellence, but it is in the way of using it where we will find the hidden key points that will give us more effectiveness in our training.

1. Interiorize the movement

When we begin to practice, all students go through a stage of being disconcerted. The body doesn't seem to respond to the mind; we emulated the movements that they teach us, we move the arms and legs thinking that we are doing the same as everyone else... but the mirror insists on contradicting us. During the process of basic learning, we divide (or at least they explain it to us like this) the movements in order to move on by dominating them step by step, and little by little we learn them. We put the letters together to make words and later we end up with phrases, until we can at last write a book. One of the most effective tricks during these stages is that of learning to interiorize the movement. To do that, one must learn to train alone, repeating the techniques with the eyes closed. We human beings are very dependent on our sense of sight for everything. By repeatedly cancelling it out, we can identify sensations that would in any other way take a long time to integrate into the group of signals that controls the brain in order to control the movement.

When a fist attack comes, it generates a series of contacts, of angulations of the trunk and the hips that give greater or lesser efficiency at their application. In hand-to-hand combat, the sense of touch is essential since one might not visually perceive what the opponent is doing while the bodies are entwined. A slight change of weight can lead to the anticipation of the next entrance in Judo, as much as a telegraphic look can do the same in a Karate attack.

Feeling the movement is not only to visualize it, but to do it in the same way that we integrate the sensations that accompany it. That information creates channels within the routes of our nervous system, highways, shortcuts, which save energy that in the end remain available to be used in the form of power and speed, or what is even more important, in the form of attention to the thousand and one variables and situations that can provoke our opponent.

The continuous practice with the eyes closed will give wings to your technique, will make it more efficient, and especially, sober. Combat is always an entropic situation where the one who saves more winds up winning since the one who endures wins.

2. "No tension, no obstruction"

The learning processes always suppose great wear and effort. This usually happens to the extent that at not knowing which muscle groups one must utilize, one ends up tensing all of them. Mastery is always measured by the fluidity of execution, by the "complicated simplicity," the natural efficiency of the practitioner.

If from the beginning you eliminate tension, you will be saving a great deal of energy and probably injuries as well. Let's take the example of an elemental technique like the front kick: in the first part of the technique, one must use the muscle groups in the front part of the legs, the quadriceps. In this moment, all tension in the antagonistic muscles, iliacus, will obstruct your action; only at the moment of complete extension should they be tense. When practicing, by using the minimum levels of tension necessary to move our extremity, we will slow down the movement; that will allow the brain to understand a complete series of implications from the rest of the body in the process. If, furthermore, we do it with the eyes closed, we will take multiple advantage, we will "feel" how our weight moves over the support leg, how the hip rises, how the trunk counter-poses our action (any other way we would fall to the floor), how the feet muscles stretch. So, concentrate on not tensing.

As in almost everything in life, our greatest enemy is ourselves. When we focus on not tensing, we stop interfering negatively, we save energy and we discover with little effort that which would take a lot longer any other way.

Contrary to the old proverb of muscle builders, "No pain, no gain," the martial artist should say, "No tension, no obstruction."

3. Train the techniques in diverse positions Why learn how to strike with a fist standing if you can do it sitting?

During the learning process, the principle of "divide and conquer" is undoubtedly one of the essential strategies.

When we train a technique in a position distinct from that which we are later going to use it, we give the central computer a chance to center its attention on only one part of the execution phases. I understand that one might feel a little ridiculous kicking while lying on the floor, or squatting, or holding onto the wall, but in each one of these positions we are isolating the principle muscles that will intervene in the technique when we apply it while standing up.

By doing this, we can concentrate much more adequately on achieving a correct application of point number two of this article, becoming real misers with our energy. Generally speaking, one then discovers the uselessness of tensing muscles groups that in the end only act as accessories in the execution of the techniques, modulating its execution instead of intervening directly, groups that the neophyte tenses inadequately, reducing speed and, as a consequence, power.

The same thing is true when at putting ourselves in a different situation from the normal one, we question the balance in a distinct way, storing data that will allow us to evaluate and manage the compensatory movements that each technique implies in the areas that are not directly involved in the execution of each technique.

Breaking the routine in training always opens new perspectives, conscious and unconscious, which will allow us to accelerate the learning.

4. The world in reverse!

Following this powerful key point already discussed of breaking with routine, I propose that you put the world in reverse. Make the attacks defense and the defense attacks. Do what you do on the upper parts of your opponent on the lower, change your right for the left, your left for your right. Turn the world upside down!

When one practices a defense technique as an attack or the contrary, one is exploring the "dark side" of the same thing, closing the circle in the mind and betting on versatility. Rapid techniques executed slowly, the slow ones executed quickly, make the circular straight and the straight circular and the range of options is almost infinite when making paradox your ally.

Seeing things from different angles offers the brain a chance to reconsider and confirm what has been learned, it gauges your abilities and generates firm support so you can be creative. If your favorite combinations begin with the arms and end with the legs, do it the opposite way; if first you try to throw forward to later take advantage of the defensive energy of the opponent going backwards, try the opposite combination; the least that will happen is that you will discover why these, and not others, are your favourites and perhaps you might even surprise yourself by surprising your partners with a creative vein that makes you disconcerting in combat.

5. Observe nature.
Apply each thing in combat

"The theory is seen in the practice" says the ancient proverb. A technique that isn't contrasted with itself in combat, like the knife that isn't used, will never sharpen.

The best techniques are those which arise from the result of pressure that the skill of a training partner exercises. When one grows tired because he always enters with the same combination, one must begin to visualize the collection of actions that will neutralize it, training it alone first, later with someone else, and finally applying it with our defiant partner to see whether it works or not.

In such a process, the purification technique reaches its greatest level of excellence; reality is always the hardest test with which we check ourselves and Mastery always arises from continuously rubbing up against it. Its arguments are always incontestable, for nature, the ultimate reality, is the only Master that never makes a mistake, for that it has always been a source of inspiration for budokas the world over. Attacking with the power of a wave breaking on the beach, striking like a lightning bolt, moving like a cat, stretching like a crane, sliding like a cloud, wrapping the opponent up like a gust of wind, strangling him like a boa constrictor... the examples are well known but to penetrate their mystery there is only one path: to train and train and train... and later... to train more, so, good training!

"Attacking with the power of a wave breaking on the beach, striking like a lightning bolt, moving like a cat, stretching like a crane, sliding like a cloud, wrapping the opponent up like a gust of wind, strangling him like a boa constrictor..."

半硬軟

INDEX